GENERAL GREELY

CAPTAIN GREELY
After the Rescue, Homeward Bound

GENERAL GREELY

The Story of a Great American

By GENERAL WILLIAM MITCHELL

* *
*
*

NEW YORK

G · P · PUTNAM'S SONS

1936

55507
920
B 794 m

PRINTED IN THE UNITED STATES OF AMERICA

AT THE VAN REES PRESS

This small work on the life of Adolphus Washington Greely is dedicated to the youth of America, who, I hope, may draw inspiration from the deeds and accomplishments of this great soldier, explorer, statesman and philosopher. It is written by one who is proud to number himself as one of his disciples.

Contents

CONTENTS

Illustrations

Introduction

IN April, 1898, while a student at college, I sat in the gallery of the United States Senate, of which my father was a member, and heard that august body declare war against Spain. That declaration meant only one thing for me and that was to go home and enlist under the flag of our country. A few days after this I became a full-fledged private in the First Wisconsin Infantry, the successor of the organization with which my father had marched to the Civil War. After serving for a short time as a private, I was discharged to accept a commission in the Signal Corps of the United States Army, which was just then being organized.

Like many boys of eighteen, I knew little about what this meant and did not relish leaving my organization, as we expected to be fighting the Spaniards in Cuba in a short time. However, orders were orders and I was assigned as a second lieutenant to the 2nd Volunteer Signal Company then being organized at Washington Barracks, D. C. As there was practically no Signal Corps when the war began, one had to be improvised at once. This important work was under the direction of General A. W. Greely, on whose recommendation I had been commissioned in the Signal

Corps. I had been acquainted with him before but after my entrance into the military service, that acquaintance ripened into respect, friendship and admiration.

This wonderful man was born at Newburyport, Massachusetts, on March 27, 1844—before Admiral Perry had opened up Japan, before the Mexican War and the acquisition of the immense territory from that republic which gave us our Pacific Coast, and long before our Pacific railroads had been constructed. When General Greely was born, many of the principal actors in the Napoleonic period in Europe were still alive. Metternich, Austria's great Chancellor, was in control of affairs in that Empire. The Emperor Francis Joseph, who reigned for sixty-eight years, had not yet ascended the throne. Queen Victoria was in her twenties.

General Greely's maternal grandfather fought in the Revolutionary War and he himself, at the age of seventeen, enlisted as a private and fought through the Civil War with marked distinction. He bore a conspicuous part in the Reconstruction days. He built thousands of miles of telegraph lines through our southwestern country in the seventies, and became the Army's expert in this field. He led a scientific expedition to the Polar regions which discovered new lands, reached the farthest north and carried out climatic and magnetic observations of the greatest importance. Abandoned for two years by the relief parties which were sent north, he maintained his organization intact for three years, although it was finally decimated by starvation and unheard of hardships until few survivors remained when relief arrived.

INTRODUCTION

It is one of the most heroic tales of tenacity and privation ever recorded.

Greely reorganized and made efficient the United States Weather Bureau. He prevailed on Professor Langley to build the first man-carrying heavier-than-air machine. He fostered aeronautics long before most people thought there was any such thing. He organized the Signal Corps of the United States Army during the Spanish War, and had direct charge of all cable censorship in this country. He located Admiral Cervera's fleet in Santiago Harbor ten days before the Navy knew where it was. He advised President McKinley to attack Santiago, Cuba, instead of Havana as had been contemplated, which resulted in a quick ending of the Spanish War.

Under his direction the Alaska telegraph system was completed, a stupendous work. He laid the first American-made deep-sea cables, when it was thought that none could be fabricated in this country. He procured the first automobiles for the army, the first radios, and put into operation the first long distance radio communication ever installed. He ended his active service in command of the United States troops at San Francisco immediately after the earthquake and fire of 1906.

His Arctic experiences made him a world celebrity. He was the confidant of many of our Presidents, and known to practically every crowned head in the world. He frequently went to Europe as a member of various commissions, scientific, geographical and military. He was one of the world's greatest geographers.

When General Greely was born, the population of the United States amounted to about 20,000,000. It is a pleasure to contemplate that in the span of a man's life all these stupendous changes have taken place in our country, and that this man was one of the great actors and one of the most forward-looking persons ever to grace our public service.

In the succeeding pages I shall tell something of Greely's experiences, from his entry in the United States Army up to his death.

In the preparation of this book, I have been greatly assisted by General Greely's family, including the General himself, and particularly by Miss Rose Greely; by General Brainard; by Mr. William Emory, son of Lieut. Emory, commander of the U.S.S. *Bear;* by Lieut. Com. Lucien Green, from whom I obtained Ensign Harlow's journal and photographs; by the Hon. Frank Marshall of Maine, who was present when the Greely party and Relief Expedition entered Portsmouth; by the Hon. F. W. Hartford, former mayor of Portsmouth, N. H., and owner of the Portsmouth *Gazette;* by Mrs. Reginald Vickers, an old friend and neighbor of the Greely family; and by Mr. R. W. Kauffmann of the Evening *Star*, Washington, D. C. To all of these I wish to express my thanks and appreciation for the time and effort they have so generously expended.

GENERAL GREELY

Chapter I

YOUTH AND YOUNG MANHOOD

FOR nine generations, three hundred years, Greely's ancestors lived and labored in New England. Since Andrew Greely, in 1639, none of his father's line had lived or died out of sight of the Cape Ann Light, except one.

His grandfather, Stephen Greely, moved from Haverhill, old home of the family, to Newburyport, and accumulated considerable wealth for that period, when a man with an income of $1,000 a year was considered rich. However, this was swept away in the fire of 1811, and he had to start again as a shoemaker. His son, John Balch Greely (General Greely's father), was brought up in this trade. A man of scholarly tastes and cultured nature, he had supplemented his common school education by much reading, and through him, young Greely early became versed in the history of his country and in public questions of the time. The elder Greely imbued him with his ideas and beliefs, such as abstention from foreign entanglements; preparedness against Europe; equal opportunities for men and women in education; abolition of slavery; religious toleration; economy, both personal and national; but above all, a sense of obligation to one's community and country, and a devotion to duty. As a boy of twelve, John Balch Greely served as a servant to an

3

officer in the War of 1812, which aroused an interest in military affairs that persisted all his life, and this interest Greely also shared. John Balch Greely died during the Civil War.

General Greely's maternal grandfather fought in the Revolutionary War, and he himself has talked with men who were soldiers in that contest. It is remarkable that there was a man alive in 1935 who had seen and known soldiers of the Revolutionary War, who served in 1776, and soldiers of the World War, who served in 1918, 143 years apart.

His mother, Frances D. Cobb, was a woman of forceful character, uncompromising integrity and rare common sense. Although a slight person, she possessed wonderful physical endurance, which Greely inherited. She was never sick a day in her life and died at eighty-one of old age. When the father's means were exhausted, after he contracted tuberculosis, she worked in a cotton mill as a weaver and supported the family comfortably. She had to rise at dawn to cook breakfast for her family, which also included an invalid stepson, a widowed mother, a sister and a young niece and nephew; then she worked ten hours in the mill, returning after dark to cook supper and attend to various other household duties. She was an insatiable reader with an inquiring mind; and notwithstanding her manifold duties, she found time for her reading, and kept up with public opinion on current topics.

Newburyport, a seaport town of ten thousand people, with a local history of more than 250 years, drew most of its

4

wealth from the sea. From its shipyards came some of the most famous sailing ships of the era, the "Dreadnaught," "Racer" and "Pride of the Seas." The stately colonial mansions up and down High Street were filled with rare porcelains, china and ornaments brought from far harbors of the world by sailing men. Fishing smacks, manned entirely by Americans, took great quantities of codfish. In the winter most of these fishermen put in their time making shoes in the small factories there. Although somewhat provincial, Newburyport was a well-educated community, with a large public library, literary societies and excellent schools. Her maritime commerce kept her in vital touch with the world.

In the forties and fifties of the last century, the conditions of daily life in the United States were much the same as they had been during Colonial times. Those of pure Anglo-Saxon strain who inhabited the thirteen original colonies still maintained the customs, religion and daily routine that their pioneer ancestors had followed. In New England this was particularly so, and men of native American strain still manned the ships, whalers, merchantmen and naval vessels that sailed the seas. The mills that were just beginning to spring up here were filled with native Americans. The same people who had wrested the land from the Indians and cultivated and developed it with their own hands were still there.

The church was still the dominating factor in the life of that time, and from it devolved most of the social activities. The people lived simple, frugal lives, with few pleasures and luxuries: lectures, concerts and church fairs in winter; boat-

5

ing, swimming, berrying and church picnics in summer, were the principal amusements. Now and then a show or circus came to town, but they were frowned on as worldly and wicked. In a community where there was so little wealth, the children had not much pocket money; Greely remembers his first earned money, gotten by weeding onions at one cent a row.

Greely was educated in the public schools. This was before the day of co-education, and the boys went to a boys' school, taught by men, where their infractions of discipline were severely punished by the rod and not by moral suasion. Children's parties were mostly all girls or all boys, which met with the full approval of the young Greely, who thought it "sissy" to attend mixed parties. The curfew bell called all children off the street at a certain hour each evening.

This sort of existence conduced to the development of strength of body and character in men, the fostering of ideals of fair play and regard for others, and produced an honest, God-fearing and patriotic citizenry. Such conditions have ceased to exist in this country, with its transition from an agricultural to an industrial state; in fact, they did not continue very long after Greely's birth. First, the gold rush to the Pacific coast took numbers of the men away. Their places on the ships were taken by Portuguese from the Cape Verde and Azores Islands; in the mills by Italians, Greeks and Slovaks; on the farms by the Germans; while the Irish wielded the pickaxes and carried the hods.

The periods of tense political excitement that gripped New

England during the fifties and sixties had a great effect on the growing boy. Such questions as slavery, rum, religion, the gold fever, unemployment, financial panics and various isms were discussed and argued continually with great fervor by practically everybody who could talk. Greely records that national politics entered his life at six years of age! At ten, he knew the political standing of every Congressman and his vote on test questions. All these influences, the schools, the church, the press, the force of example, inculcated into the impressionable boy the ideal of giving the best he had in him to his country.

When Fort Sumter was fired on, and the President issued his call for volunteers, Greely, then a tall, upstanding boy of seventeen, attempted to enlist, but being under age was refused three times by the recruiting officers, the last of whom enraged him by saying contemptuously, "No, no, we want men, not little boys." Determined to enlist and yet not wishing to outrage his New England conscience by an out-and-out lie, Greely hit upon a satisfactory subterfuge. He went home, chalked the number 18 on the soles of his shoes, and again applied for enlistment, this time in the neighboring town of Newbury. When the recruiting officer asked him his age, he replied, "I am over eighteen," and was taken into the service and assigned to Company D, 19th Massachusetts Volunteer Infantry.

The Massachusetts troops at that time were probably as well-officered and well-equipped for field service as any that entered the war. In a month, by constant drilling, this raw

7

material had been whipped into such shape that they could march, and handle their weapons to some extent.

In the late summer, the regiment proceeded to Washington, D. C., via New York, Philadelphia and Baltimore. In New York they were received with acclamation and in Philadelphia they were entertained generously, but in Baltimore they were met with hostility. Sullen looks, menacing gestures and insulting remarks greeted them from all sides. It was but a short time since a Massachusetts regiment had been attacked there while passing through the streets.

From Baltimore they proceeded to Washington in uncovered freight cars and camped almost under the shadow of the Capitol. At that time the Capitol building was unfinished. The present dome was not on it, and the ground was littered up with building material of all kinds.

The soldiers were given passes from time to time. Many loitered around the White House, trying to get a glimpse of President Lincoln, in which young Greely was successful. He also saw General Winfield Scott in his old age, as he shuffled slowly back and forth between the White House and the War Office.

Those around the President were fearful that the Capital would be taken by the Confederates. Men were poured into the city from all directions, with and without arms, uniforms, equipment and discipline. As soon as possible, they were sent out to points along the Potomac River. The 19th Massachusetts was put in camp near Darnestown, Maryland, as a part of the Corps of Observation under General Stone. It

8

was in this locality that the call of the sentinels, "All's quiet along the Potomac," rang out through the nation and became a set phrase.

General McClellan took command of the Army and started in a rigorous system of drills, maneuvers and lectures which eventually formed the Army of the Potomac into one of the greatest fighting machines the world has ever seen.

Greely's first duty against a supposed enemy was when he was ordered down along the towpath of the Chesapeake and Ohio Canal to resist an attack said to be coming from the other side of the Potomac. Ammunition was issued, but few knew how to load their muskets properly. One man asked, "Which end of the bullet do I put in the muzzle?" (All weapons at that time were muzzle loaders.) Some one answered, "Why, the pointed end, you fool," and they went ahead and loaded them that way. No attack came. When they got back to camp, they went out to the firing range, where targets were put up about fifty yards away. The men who had put their bullets in wrong end first were badly battered up by the kick of the muskets.

The regiments were scattered out, not yet being gathered up into brigades, but there was a good deal of visiting between them. Men from New York, Michigan, Minnesota and other states met for the first time and discussed their common mission. It was a great breeder of nationalism.

Greely's first actual field service occurred in October, 1861, when an abortive attempt was made to capture Leesburg, Virginia. The engagement was known as the battle

9

of Ball's Bluff, and was one of the worst fiascoes of the war. The movement started from the north side of the Potomac River along the towpath of the Chesapeake and Ohio canal. The troops first crossed to Harrison's Island in the Potomac, five hundred yards from the Maryland shore and about two hundred yards from the Virginia side. This island is about two miles long and three hundred yards wide. Both crossings were difficult, due to heavy rains. Greely's company was put to work as boatmen and pioneers in two cumbersome flat-boats that had been dragged down from the canal. Fifty men went over at a time. There were no oars, so the boats had to be poled back and forth.

Soon the fire of musketry began across the river, at first a long way off, then gradually drawing nearer. Wounded and dying men began to be ferried back from the Virginia shore. As Greely's boat neared Harrison's Island, it met another boat carrying the body of Colonel Baker of the First California Regiment, Senator-elect from Oregon, who had been killed leading the United States forces. This had a depressing effect on the young soldiers who had not yet received their baptism of fire. Proceeding further, they were greeted by various wounded men with the cries: "No one has escaped, every one is dead, wounded or a prisoner! Go back, you are facing sure death!" Seasoned soldiers are used to these expressions from men who have left the fighting lines for one cause or another, as they do not wish to belittle themselves to their comrades. It always makes a strong impression on young soldiers, however. When Greely crossed the island

and faced the Virginia shore, he came in full sight of the battle going on there. The bluff, densely wooded, rose sheer from the river for over one hundred feet, with practically no roads or trails up its face. The Confederates had stationed themselves on the crest. Had they charged down upon the remnant of Union soldiers on the Virginia side, they would have killed them all. Greely's company kept up a desultory fire whenever the enemy showed themselves.

One leaky scow still went back and forth for the wounded. As it landed for the last time on the Virginia side, there was a rush of panic-stricken men who filled it to overflowing, leaving many behind. Half-way across an accident occurred, the boat was swamped and the river was filled with struggling men, some of whom reached the island while others were swept away by the current. As darkness approached, an occasional soldier swam across to the island from the Virginia shore. That night it rained hard, turning their camp into a muddy quagmire. The young soldiers were getting a real initiation into war. There was no order or cohesion in the command, each company shifting for itself.

Greely's company was detailed to bury the dead on the battlefield and look after the wounded on the island, under a flag of truce which the Confederates granted. The naked and half-clad bodies in their death pallor, dirty and horrible, with gaping wounds, were not a heartening sight. Greely remembered one man's body in particular. He was clothed only in trousers and covered with mud and slime. His mouth was open and blood oozed from a wound in his forehead, where he had been shot as he climbed out of the river after swimming across. As he was picked up for burial, one of the men said, "He is alive. I saw him move his lips." But another shouted, "Take him along with the others, he will never get over it." At this Captain Mahoney interfered, furious at such ruthlessness. "You damned brute," he cried, "I would like to kill you for that! You will have to bury me first." Eventually the unconscious man was taken back to the Maryland shore and put in the hospital, where he fully recovered.

The Confederates had been almost as unprepared to resist the attack as the Federals had been to make it. Several of the Union sharpshooters had been so near Leesburg that they could see the church towers through the telescopic sights with which their rifles were equipped. Next day the Union troops left the island and went back to their camp life. They had found out something about what war meant.

The topography of the battlefield of Ball's Bluff is much the same today as it was then. A stone marker points to the top of the bluff where the Colonel of a Pennsylvania regiment was killed leading his men. Facing this is the grave of Captain Hatcher of the Virginia troops who died in the defense of his native state. Alongside is a little Union cemetery, surrounded by a round stone wall, with a tall flagpole carrying the national colors in the center. Within are forty-two graves, one known, forty-one unknown.

The American volunteers were men of exceptional intelligence and they began at once to size up their officers and discuss matters of tactics and strategy. They seriously questioned the capacity of their generals to lead them, and began to realize also that although many of their officers were good disciplinarians and drill masters, they knew almost nothing of actual war conditions.

The 19th Massachusetts now moved to Great Falls on the Potomac, to protect the reservoir for the water supply of Washington. Greely had been promoted to be corporal and was put in command of one of a series of three-man picket posts established up and down the river about a mile apart. He was still seventeen, a tall, lanky boy, grave, clear-headed and cool. The men with him were over thirty. Thus he spent the winter of 1861-62 with his company, camped in dog tents and short of much necessary equipment, including shoes.

By the spring of 1862, General McClellan had got some semblance of organization into the Army of the Potomac. The plan of operations was for this Army to proceed to the York Peninsula, via Fortress Monroe and Yorktown, and from there advance on Richmond, the capital of the Confederacy. Greely's regiment was detailed as part of a force to proceed up the Shenandoah Valley in Virginia to act as a diversion for McClellan, who had gone to the York Peninsula. This movement amounted to little, merely marching and countermarching. The population of this part of Virginia consisted only of very old men, young boys, women and children, as all the men of fighting age were with the Confederate forces. It was at Charlestown in this vicinity that John Brown had been hung for attempting to cause an uprising among the slaves. Greely remembered that it caused much resentment when the Union bands marched about playing "John Brown's Body Lies a-Mouldering in the Grave," with the soldiers singing the refrain.

Soon the regiment marched back to Washington, and on March 27th, Greely's eighteenth birthday, embarked for the Peninsula. The boat furnished them was so unseaworthy that the troops had to be debarked at Point Lookout, Maryland, at the mouth of the river, and taken on board another vessel. When they reached Fortress Monroe, the *Monitor* was lying close by. It had defeated the Confederate ram, *Merrimac*, only a month before and so made the Peninsula campaign possible. It was so little and insignificant looking that the men could hardly believe it had had such an effect.

Greely's regiment started out by leading the advance of the Union Army. They incurred their first casualties at the siege of Yorktown. Nearly every day now brought them into contact with the enemy, and they became used to both artillery and infantry fire. In those days the artillery projectiles traveled so slowly that sentinels were posted to watch for batteries firing. When they saw the flash of the guns, they yelled "Down," and the men rushed for cover in the interior ditch of their trench. When the projectile had passed over, they resumed their ordinary duties. Seldom was a man hit.

Gradually siege works were pushed against Yorktown and it was there that the first American balloon under Professor Lowe ascended into the air. It obtained valuable information about the dispositions of the Confederate forces. General

Heintzleman of the Union Army was the first general officer to make an ascent in this aircraft. It is a matter of interest that his grandson, the present General Heintzleman, was the first of our general staff officers to fly over the enemy lines in Europe. I myself piloted him.

During the Yorktown siege, Count Ferdinand von Zeppelin, then a Lieutenant of Prussian Cavalry, was attached to General McClellan's headquarters. He had been with Professor Lowe at Minneapolis, Minnesota, where the balloon detachment was organized, and was with the professor frequently during the Peninsula campaign. It was there that he gained his inspiration which later took form and developed the wonderful Zeppelin airships of today.

When the Confederates saw the siege preparations, they evacuated Yorktown without a battle. The campaign of the Chickahominy followed, during which the Union Army lived for weeks in the swamps. Here the young soldiers were attacked by wood ticks on the land and moccasin snakes in the water, while the malaria fever killed or permanently disabled many a good man. But they toiled on, wet and weary, without change of clothing or dry bedding at night. Little was known of malaria at that time, and to counteract it the doctors issued whisky and quinine.

At the battle of Fair Oaks, Greely's organization held the first line rifle pits only three and a half miles from Richmond. Several battles had occurred there before, and the dead had been buried in shallow graves. Heavy rains fell and partially washed the bodies up. Dead animals lay strewn around the ground, and in the heat of June, the stench from all this was terrible. The putrefying animal matter poisoned the water, which had to be boiled before it was fit for drinking. Food in any quantity was hard to obtain, and rations consisted principally of hard-tack, bacon and coffee.

With the two armies actually in contact all the time and firing going on almost continually, there was little rest for the soldiers. For weeks neither clothing nor accouterments were removed, night or day. Men lay down in their shelter tents placed in rows, with their muskets stacked in front of these company streets. The army was always ready for surprise attacks. One can imagine the condition of the men's bodies after a short space of time under such circumstances. Death and disease decimated the organization, but Greely's vigorous constitution kept him fit for duty. He was always careful to follow the rules issued by the surgeon for health and sanitation.

At Oak Grove, on June 25th, Greely's regiment was detailed in reserve in some woods on the right of Heintzleman's Division, and told not to fire unless ordered to attack. Confederate forces came into the other end of the woods and opened fire, but such was the discipline of the 19th Massachusetts that although forty-three men were killed and wounded, not a shot was fired in return. The Confederates, thinking the woods unoccupied, advanced to the attack but they were received by such a warm defense by Greely's regiment, now ordered to fire, that they had to retreat. The repelling of this attack was greatly helped by the use of an experimental cartridge which had just been issued. The powder was attached to the rear end of the bullet in a piece of glazed paper, and this could be dropped right into the bore of the musket without the necessity of ramming, thereby greatly increasing the rate of fire.

The Ordnance Department thought this too complicated a device to issue to the army, together with the repeating rifle which at that time had been invented, so these were not issued, until toward the end of the war. Young Greely noticed this, and it undoubtedly impressed him deeply with the detrimental effects of military conservatism that is sometimes carried to a point where it causes disaster.

The men in the ranks thought they were going to move forward to take Richmond and end the war. They were enthusiastic; but to their disgust, there came an announcement that a strategic movement to a new base on the James River was to be made. The men instantly realized this was to be a disgraceful retreat, and were in a fury. They had fought for three months to gain a position close to Richmond which they knew they could hold. They were so near the city they could hear its church bells ringing. Now after their terrible campaign, their heavy losses in battle and a forty per cent loss by disease, they were to make an ignominious retreat.

All day long a constant stream of troops and wagons moved eastward toward the James River. All equipment and supplies that could not be carried along were to be destroyed. Enormous quantities of excellent material, worth millions of dollars, were piled up and burned. Ammunition dumps were blown up. A train of cars, loaded with supplies, was driven through an open bridge into the river, as that was the easiest way of destroying it. The soldiers did not understand what was going on but they well knew that some one had made a terrible blunder. While they were marching with the shortest kind of rations, they saw before their eyes thousands of full rations consumed in flames.

Soon the Confederates, apprised of the retreat, began a general attack all along the line. Greely's regiment was detailed to the rearguard of the organization, and for a few days was involved in practically continuous skirmishing, marching, repelling and making attacks, in order to cover the movement. Vegetation was so thick and the woods so dense that often the men engaged in hand-to-hand fighting with sword and bayonet.

In one of the encounters, Greely was wounded in the leg, while another bullet disabled his rifle. It was his first wound in the Civil War. On that day his regiment suffered a loss of twenty-five officers and men killed, and seventy-seven wounded. Greely did not enter his wound on the list of casualties, but kept right on with it. The retreat was so rapid that the dead and dying had to be left on the field.

They reached Malvern Hill about daybreak, having marched all night, and Greely saw the main attack of the Confederate army across open ground against the Union position. The Confederate charges were of a desperate character and most gallantly carried out. They surged up the hill with colors flying, bands playing and men cheering, covered not only with the musketry fire of the Union infantry but also the heavy artillery fire from batteries deployed between the infantry and from gunboats on the James River.

How different a battlefield of that period from a modern one! Nowadays, almost no men are seen. Fire from machine guns and field pieces is not followed by smoke. The only dust and smoke one sees is that thrown up by the impact of bursting shells. In the Civil War, the battlefields were covered with dense, opaque, sulphurous smoke which hung heavy and close if no wind was blowing. Troops advanced in lines two deep, the men shoulder to shoulder, with their color-bearers out in front. At two or three hundred yards they fired, and advanced by rushes. If they could sustain the advance, when within one hundred yards of the enemy they fired several volleys, fixed bayonets and charged. The artillery kept with the infantry, going into action in the intervals between the troops.

On this day, General Sedgwick, the division commander, saw Greely limping along with his wounded leg, and without a weapon. He asked, "What are you doing there without a gun?" Greely saluted and said, "My rifle was broken by a bullet last night when I was also wounded. I have stayed with my company and will take a rifle from the first man wounded today." "That is right," said General Sedgwick, pleased with this soldierly fortitude, "I will give you an Enfield rifle myself." He obtained one and personally handed it to Greely. It was a fine light weapon with a beautiful stock, which Greely carried until he was badly wounded at Antietam, when it passed to another man.

General Sedgwick was highly regarded by soldiers and officers alike both as a tactician and a strategist. Unfortunately he was killed later in the Wilderness, by a sharpshooter, while riding across an open space in fancied security. The sharpshooter was up a tree, concealed by its branches. I have been to the spot and as I remember it, the distance was nearly five hundred yards, a long shot in those days.

Chapter II

BATTLES OF A BOY SOLDIER

POSTED on Malvern Hill, Greely's company soon came under the Confederate artillery fire, which forced their withdrawal behind the crest. As darkness came, the firing ceased and the battle was over. All they had for dinner was hardtack. There was no water or fuel; but after their days of marching and fighting, without sleep, any respite was welcome. Men fell down fast asleep and remained there like logs.

Midnight marching orders came again, accompanied by heavy rains which usually follow a battle. Men marched in their sleep. No one knew where they were going. The roads were full of infantry, cavalry and artillery, with columns crossing each other and at times colliding and creating great confusion. At last with the breaking dawn they reached Harrison's Landing on the James River, where they went into camp on the rain-soaked earth. The mud was so thick and caked so heavily that many of the men cut off their trousers at the knee and with bare legs and feet went about their duties.

At Harrison's Landing, General McClellan rode among the men, making speeches, in an attempt to encourage them. His soldiers had a great regard for McClellan, but many of them felt very resentful toward him for not having made a more serious effort to capture Richmond. A much more enthusiastic reception was accorded to President Lincoln, when he visited the army a few days later. He was cheered wherever he went. The loyalty and discipline of the Army of the Potomac had not been broken, but their chagrin at their unsuccessful campaign was tremendous.

In ten months, Greely's regiment had lost more than fifty per cent of its effective strength, killed, wounded, diseased, prisoners or sick. The army remained at Harrison's Landing, a prey to all sorts of rumors. The Confederate forces constantly harassed them; one week passed into another, and the talk of "On to Richmond" died down. Finally, orders were received to destroy all food and equipment that could not be carried, and to move to Newport News.

On this march the soldiers were allowed to take vegetables, cattle, hogs, poultry or anything they could get from the country, in an attempt to reduce the enemy's supplies. On their first advance up the Peninsula they had been forbidden to touch a thing, but war was now becoming less polite.

After a few days at Newport News, Greely's command was placed on a boat, bound ostensibly for Washington. The capacity of the boat was five or six hundred men, but over two thousand were put aboard. It was so crowded they could not take exercise, or even sleep. They went aboard with one day's rations, and the trip lasted four days. Instead of going to Washington, they were debarked at Alexandria, on August 27, 1862. No sooner had they landed than they heard that General Pope's army, then south of Manassas, Virginia, was having a hard time.

Then came the news that Pope was in ignominious retreat and orders were received that the troops at Alexandria should march at once to Centreville, Virginia. The brigade commander protested that the men were physically exhausted, in a state of semi-starvation and could not move, so a respite of seven hours was granted them. Then they began a terrific march. Conflicting orders caused them to go fifty miles out of their way, so when they got to Fairfax, Virginia, they had marched 63 miles in 64 consecutive hours, twenty-four of which were in a heavy rain which made the sticky red gumbo of the roads very hard to negotiate. The Confederate partisan troops, Mosby's men, were operating through this vicinity, and frequent alarms were given, which caused the troops to form line and await attack several times. However, practically all the men reached Fairfax, as a battle was in prospect. How different were these volunteers of '61 and '62 from the conscripts and bounty-jumpers of 1864, who had to be herded up at the point of the bayonet.

From Fairfax they moved to Chantilly, where Stonewall Jackson had thrown back the repeated assaults of the Union troops. Here they heard that Generals Phil Kearny and Stevens had been killed. Both these officers had been considered as possible successors to General McClellan, in command of the Army, as his relief had been decided upon. Had they lived and been so appointed, there might never have been a General Grant.

The remnants of Pope's army were saved by McClellan, and they fell back to the defenses of Washington. In this campaign, the command of a new army unit known as the "Army of Virginia" was given to General Pope, whose principal qualification for that high office was that he had been digging an artesian well in Texas. Pope started off by issuing a bombastic order, dated "Headquarters in the Saddle." In it he pointed out that the troops in the west were used to seeing the rebel soldiers' backs, not their faces. Now he, General Pope, had come to lead the Easterners to victory. This braggadocio was badly taken by the troops who had been up against the wonderful Confederate Army of Northern Virginia. The soldiers nicknamed Pope "Hindquarters in the Saddle," and had little respect for him. General Lee, turning from McClellan's army on the Peninsula, had attacked Pope's army near Sperryville and sent General Stonewall Jackson with a few thousand men clear around and behind him, one of the most brilliant operations of a detachment on the flank of a main army that ever occurred. Had McClellan's army not come to the relief of Pope when it did, the "Army of Virginia" would have been utterly destroyed by Lee's forces. At this time, the Confederates came nearer destroying and capturing a whole Union army than at any period in the war.

Greely's organization was in the rear guard, covering the corps of Porter, Sigel and Sumner. With the 19th Massachusetts was the First Minnesota and a Rhode Island battery. The Confederates followed up closely and kept firing on their retreating columns. In this retreat, organizations ran into each other at night and opened fire, stampeded and went through all the mishaps that invariably accompany a disorderly retreat. Back in the lines near Washington, the 19th Massachusetts was promised garrison duty and the men looked forward to some rest and recuperation, but that was not to be. It was one of the few Union regiments kept in the field constantly during the whole war, being listed among the famous "300 Fighting Regiments of the Civil War." The men never knew the comfort of a permanent camp or garrison.

Greely was now a seasoned soldier, had been wounded in battle, displayed conspicuous gallantry on many occasions, and was only eighteen years old. Already he was looked up to and respected as a man experienced in war, cool in emergencies and strong on the march.

The regiment crossed over to the Maryland side, where they received their first mail in several weeks. Here it was filled by recruits who it was hoped could be broken in and accustomed to the regimental routine before another battle was undertaken; but General Lee was advancing north and Harpers Ferry had been captured. On came the Confederates, spurred by the victory of the Second Manassas, intent on gaining a still greater victory on northern soil and possibly capturing the Federal capital. This they hoped would get them recognition from England and France, loans of money and additional supplies from foreign countries. That would have been a terrible blow to the North, not only to its military organization but to the prestige of the government.

The Army of the Potomac was sent to interpose between Lee and the capital. Greely marched with his regiment through Frederick, Maryland, where Jackson had led his troops a short time before, and where Barbara Frietchie was supposed to have waved a Union flag at him—the inspiration for Whittier's poem. Although the Army of the Potomac had advanced far beyond the status of an organized mob, it was not yet the smoothly running war machine that it became later. Disputes frequently took place between the commanders as to how they should proceed. Greely heard an altercation of this kind between Generals Sumner and Hooker, which did not add to the confidence of the men in their commanders. The enlisted men knew a great deal about what was transpiring, and when unnecessary delays occurred, they knew some one had erred.

The Confederate Army was gathering at Sharpsburg, and at 2 A.M. on September 17th, Greely's regiment had their breakfast of hardtack and coffee and the attack begun. This terrific battle, Antietam, one of the bloodiest of the whole Civil War, consisted of piecemeal attacks by the Union Army against the Confederate position, the center of which was in a sunken road. Union troops were thrown against them in masses, first on one side, then the other, then the center, with no coördination or system. They were mowed down by the Confederate fire, which was concentrated on each detachment as it attacked. While the 19th Massachu-

26

setts was in the brigade support and occupying the crest of a ledge, lying concealed, with orders that no one stand up, Greely saw a Confederate column charging down a ravine within forty yards of the flank of the front line. Realizing the vital importance of checking this, Greely rose up and shouted, "The rebels are attacking and breaking through our front line." His captain called out, "Lie down or I'll shoot you." But he persisted in standing up and calling, and word was passed on down to the colonel, with the result that the regiment changed front and the First Minnesota next to them did likewise. It stopped the flank move and served as a rallying point for the regiments broken by the Confederate assault. This independent action by the regimental commanders was cited by McClellan in his official report as having saved his army from serious disaster.

Just after this occurrence, Greely was shot in the face, the bullet cracking his jaw and knocking out several teeth. He was left on the ground as the regiment retreated. When he recovered consciousness and got up, a Confederate soldier attempted to capture him, but he got away, only to be struck in the thigh a moment later by another bullet, which knocked him down. Confederates surrounded him on practically every side, but he saw a Union battery, Rickett's, firing down a ravine, and conceived the idea of making his way up the ravine, under the shell fire. It was a desperate chance but it enabled him to escape. He made his way unaided to a field hospital station, where he received first aid. Next day, at the field hospital young Greely saw another phase of the horrors of war. There were many wounded here, both Union and Confederate, and against the side of the house, amputated arms and legs were piled up like cordwood.

Sedgwick's division, of which Greely's regiment was a part, went into the battle of Antietam with 5,000 men and lost 2,200, the General himself being wounded. The 19th Massachusetts lost 136 men out of 384 engaged, including all three of its field officers, but the organization lost neither a color nor a gun. The Union losses on that day were 12,410, the greatest of any single day in the Civil War. The loss at Shiloh in two days was 13,047. The Union Army did not follow up the attack next day, and the Confederates fell back across the Potomac unpursued.

Greely was sent to a hospital in Harrisburg, Penna., where he received the best care and attention possible. After only a month, he requested and was given a discharge from the hospital, although he was not entirely cured, but his anxiety to rejoin his command triumphed over every other feeling. Sent to Washington with a group of convalescents, he was thrown for the first time with the riffraff of the country, who had been sent up to join the army—drunks, thieves, men absent without leave, general nondescripts, dirty and undisciplined, who had to be ruled with a rod of iron.

The Union armies had been recruited to begin with by volunteer enlistment. These soldiers were the pick of the country and represented everything we like to think of as American. When volunteer enlistments began to fall off, an attempt was made to recruit the army by issuing bounties in money. Later men who were drawn to go into the service were allowed to hire a substitute. These things were pernicious in the extreme. Unprincipled men would get the bounty, then run away and "jump" it. Sometimes they were caught and put in the service, but frequently men would get a bounty two or three times, jumping it each time. These men had to be herded up like cattle under the rifles and bayonets of a guard. When they attempted to escape they were shot without mercy.

The punishments meted out to them seem cruel and inhuman today. One form of punishment, used for minor offenses, was called "riding the wooden horse." Holes were bored into a smooth log, into which four long poles were inserted, and when stood upright the log was about ten feet above the ground. A ladder was placed at each end, which reached to the body of the "horse." The offender, with a placard on his back, showing what he was there for, such as stealing, lying, fighting, etc., would have to sit on the horse. For the first hour or so, he felt little discomfort, but then his legs began to grow heavy, his knees pained and he would get feverish and thirsty. A number of men would be placed on the log at the same time and left there in some cases for many hours. When they came down, they would be hardly able to walk for a while. It usually cured them, temporarily at least, of any desire to misbehave themselves. To attempt to evade this punishment or run away meant death, as the sentinels on guard had orders to kill.

Another form of punishment was called "tying to the

wheel." The caissons of the artillery carried a spare wheel on an axle up behind them, the wheel being inclined at an angle of about forty-five degrees. The culprit was marched to the spare wheel and a gag put on him, consisting of a stick through the mouth tied firmly with a cloth behind his head. He was then placed on top of the wheel on his back, one hand tied to the felloe of the wheel and the other tied three spokes over from the first. His feet were tied to the felloe of the wheel on the opposite side separated by three spokes. When lying at an angle of forty-five degrees it was bad enough but when the wheel was given a half turn and the man's weight had to be supported by one wrist and one ankle, the pain was excruciating and most men fainted before the punishment was completed. Sometimes they would be left on the wheel for six hours or more. Being tied up once was sufficient for the average man.

"Tying on the rack" was a more severe punishment than the wheel. On the back of the battery wagons of the artillery was a heavy forage rack, with an edge about one inch thick. The offender was gagged and his hands dragged as far forward as they could be without lifting his feet from the ground and then bound to the felloes of the wheel. One foot was lifted and bound to the felloe of one wheel and the other foot to the other wheel. Thus his weight was thrown on his chest, which hung against the sharp edge of the rack. Men could stand this only a few minutes. It was the most brutal punishment given. They often begged to be killed rather than go through this terrible torture.

Bucking and gagging was one of the mildest punishments. The man was gagged, his hands drawn forward and tied in front of his shins, and a heavy stick pushed under his knees and over his arms. In this position he could hurt neither himself nor any one else. This was the usual punishment meted out to drunks.

Sometimes a man was tied up to a branch of a tree by the thumbs, lifted up until his toes just touched the ground and left there until he became tractable. Another punishment was carrying a heavy stick of cordwood on the shoulder, marching up and down before a sentinel hour by hour. A piece of wood that weighed only a couple of pounds at sunrise would feel like two hundred by midday.

No such punishments are meted out to troops nowadays, as milder forms have been found to be adequate.

The great majority of the bounty jumpers were of the criminal class. They would fight among themselves, bully others, but at heart they were cowards and cringed at the thought of really facing an enemy. A few did well after they reached the front, but very few.

On the other hand, the Confederates adopted a system of conscription from the beginning. The able-bodied men of their population were drawn by lot in a regular manner. Most of the labor along their lines of communication was done by slaves. In our World War we took a page from our experience in the Civil War and adopted conscription from the beginning, which made a great difference in the quality of the men obtained.

When Greely left the hospital, his regiment was south of the Potomac River. From Washington he was sent to Harpers Ferry, from where he made his way on his own initiative across Bolivar Heights, rejoining his regiment in the Loudoun valley on October 31st. Ten days after this General McClellan was relieved and the command of the Army of the Potomac given to General Burnside. As McClellan rode among his troops to bid them farewell, he was greeted with thunderous and prolonged cheers; but many in the ranks knew that with McClellan they had never won a victory and probably never would.

Although Burnside did not want the command and frankly told his superiors that he did not feel himself qualified for it, it was forced on him. Lee's army had fallen back south of the Rappahannock. Burnside immediately ordered his army to Falmouth, opposite Fredericksburg on the Rappahannock. The march of forty miles was made in three days, through ice and snow and over frozen roads. Many of the men had no shoes or socks. The army had not been reequipped after Antietam and was short of overcoats, blankets, tents, canteens, but had to get along as best it could.

At Falmouth, Burnside, instead of crossing at once and seizing the city, began dilly-dallying himself. During this time, General Lee occupied Fredericksburg and fortified the heights behind and on each side of the city. The Union army was then filled up to 100,000 effectives and gradually supplied with all the necessary material of war and camp equipage.

The enlisted men were impatient to attack as they wanted to see the end of the war. Finally on December 11, 1862, a bitterly cold and snowy day, the order was given to move forward. Sedgwick's plan of operations was to cross the Rappahannock in two places, one at Fredericksburg and another below it. This was in the face of Lee's veteran army thoroughly entrenched on the heights a few hundred yards back from the river and commanding every line of approach. Along the line of hills north of the river, the Union side, the greatest battery of artillery ever seen in war up to that time was assembled. There were 200 guns on these heights, and 250 distributed at other places, making a total of 450 cannon to begin the bombardment to cover the assault.

In front of Fredericksburg, the Union troops set about building a pontoon bridge, with the greatest speed and least noise, under cover of a heavy fog. However, the Confederates heard the work and opened fire on them. So effective was this fire that every man who stepped on the bridge was either killed or wounded. All the Union artillery opened on the town but failed to stop the enemy fire, so the Confederates continued to hold Fredericksburg.

Word was received that the Union troops had crossed the river below the town, and it was decided to attempt a crossing by individual boats. Volunteers were called for from Greely's brigade to man the boats, and orders were given for the volunteers from the Michigan regiment to go ahead with the 19th Massachusetts, as support. Greely scrambled

33

into one of the boats and as they pushed off into the current, the whole Union artillery opened up on the city to cover this movement.

Lieut. Claffey, commanding the boat in which Greely crossed, ordered that none but men of Company B should get into the boat. Just as they pushed off, a strange young man jumped in. Claffey ordered, "Throw him overboard." Greely and another man seized him to carry out the order, when the stranger cried, "Don't you remember me, Claffey? I am Fuller, chaplain of the 16th Massachusetts." "Go back to your regiment," roared Claffey. "We don't want chaplains here." At this Fuller said, beseechingly, "I resigned for bad health and there was talk that I was leaving the men as a battle was to be faced. I have come here as a man to fight. Let me go on." They let him stay in the boat, and an hour later he was dead in the streets of Fredericksburg. By his side lay a rifle he had taken from a man wounded in the crossing.

This river crossing was one of the most desperate attempts ever made in a battle, but they forced their way, jumped out of the boats and beating down the gallant opposition against them, got a foothold in the city. Greely's company was ordered to push up the main street and hold it at all costs until the pontoon bridge was finished. In no time, the organization was swept with fire from the front and both flanks, from houses, streets, gardens and roofs, at which they were ordered to fall back to the next block of buildings. Greely's cap was shot from his head and his left hand wounded. When they fell back, it was found that ten out of thirty combatants had been lost. Confederate soldiers occupied each end of the street, so the only escape was through a yard. Just as Greely and a companion were making their way through it, a Confederate jumped out of the house, and began to load his gun rapidly. Greely saw a wall five feet high in front of him, and as he was a great sprinter, he made for it, threw his rifle over and jumped the wall, landing on the other side just as a shot rang out behind him. His companion had been shot in the leg as he tried to scramble over.

The remainder of the company rallied and fought from house to house, vainly attempting to hold the town as ordered. Individual deeds of great valor marked the progress of the combat. At last the bridge was completed. The forlorn hope had held the bridgehead. The first organization to cross and come up the street was the 20th Massachusetts. With foolhardy courage and against the shouted warnings of the 7th Michigan and the 19th Massachusetts, they marched up the street in column of platoon fronts, with no apparent object in view, instead of deploying as skirmishers and fighting from house to house. Confederates occupied every nook and cranny on both sides and ends of the street. The advance of the Union troops was lighted up by the flash of Confederate muskets from windows and doorways, and within ten minutes, when less than a block had been covered, 97 men of the 20th had been killed or wounded. The regiment had to break and run for cover, but they held on during the cold night without food or blankets. They built fires from the remnants of furniture in the houses that had been shattered by the shells. Union and Confederate dead filled the streets and houses.

Fighting went on for two days, when the charge was made by Union troops across open ground against Marye's Heights just south of Fredericksburg, one of the most futile and sanguinary attacks ever recorded in military history. The Confederates occupied a sunken road, with trenches and rifle pits, supported by artillery, entrenched with breastworks and redoubts. The Union troops had to advance over 400 yards of open ground, subjected to terrific fire. Greely's regiment had eight out of eleven color bearers killed in this advance.

In the retirement, Greely's regiment was the last to cross the river. His Company, B of the 19th Massachusetts, had been first in the city and the last to get out. Out of 300 men that this regiment carried into the fight, 108 were killed or wounded. Greely, although wounded, kept with his company. For his work in this fight, Greely was promoted from corporal to sergeant.

After this, the "stick-in-the-mud" fiasco occurred, in January, 1863, when Burnside attempted to move the army to the fords above Fredericksburg, which of course should have been done in December. The mud was so bad that the army was unable to make it. The day after the failure,

Greely was in command of the extreme westerly outpost. General Burnside rode by, followed by his staff, all spattered with mud. Greely turned out his guard and gave him the salute. He and his men noted how sad and worn Burnside looked, and pitied him deeply.

January, 1863, marked the end of Greely's service with the Army of the Potomac. Within those twenty months, a heterogeneous mob of American citizens, knowing nothing of military procedure, discipline or coördinated action, had been transformed by General McClellan into a disciplined army, trained in every phase of the art possible in that short time. It had been constantly in the field, fought innumerable battles and stood some of the greatest losses ever recorded. In spite of failures, it had engendered in the men the spirit of invincibility which never left them.

The men who composed this army, also that of the Confederates, were the most intelligent ever brought together in war up to this time. Not bound by old traditions and systems as were the armies of continental Europe, they had evolved a system of war of their own, so far ahead of anything else ever thought of that there was no comparison. The Union front then extended for 2,000 miles, from the mouth of Chesapeake Bay on the Atlantic to the Gulf of Mexico in Texas. Along the outer rim of this arc were deployed about 1,000,000 men, while the Confederates, with the interior line on the other side, had about 600,000.

In February, 1863, furloughs were given to two men in

each company and Greely was one of them in Company B. Upon his return, it was intended to make him a lieutenant in the 19th Massachusetts. During his service in that regiment, he had never missed a fight and had never been absent except on account of wounds.

Chapter III

SERVICE IN THE WEST

WHILE Greely was at his home in Massachusetts, he was offered a commission in a regiment of Negroes just being formed, and as this was very flattering to a boy only eighteen years old, he accepted it. He was mustered into the 81st Colored Infantry. The men for this regiment were in Louisiana, so the officers were sent there from New York by sea, as the Mississippi was closed by the Confederates at Vicksburg and Port Hudson.

Proceeding to Baton Rouge, they organized the Negro companies from free colored men of that locality and refugee Negroes from Alabama, Louisiana and Mississippi. With these companies they engaged later in the siege of Port Hudson, which they occupied after its surrender, until sent to New Orleans as a garrison after the war, 1865 to 1867.

Greely had risen to be a captain and brevet-major before he was twenty-one, and had always served with his regiment. The colored troops were new to their officers but they found the ex-slaves clean, obedient, sober and hard working. Many of these Negroes were very religious, but their beliefs were warped by mysticism, superstition, dream-revelations and voodoism. Much of their leisure time was passed in religious

39

gatherings, where those who groaned the loudest and gesticulated most wildly were given credit for possessing the highest spiritual qualities. Their hymns, characterized by the monotonous African rhythm and sung in a wailing minor key, were new to Greely. He was especially impressed by one, the refrain of which he remembered all his life:

> "And they drove ten-penny nails all through Him,
> Hallowed be His Name."

One of the soldiers, who was a well-known preacher of high standing among his people, acted in a very sinful way during the day, and when called to account for it by Greely, he said, "Religion does not mean that I must never lie, steal or commit other sins. If we were all perfect in every way the great glory of sweet Jesus is gone. He came to save sinners, and to be saved by Jesus we must sin and then repent, and I do both. When we repent Jesus takes us into His bosom as lost lambs."

While on duty in New Orleans, in 1866, Greely went through a terrible epidemic of smallpox and yellow fever, which struck terror into the hearts of the soldiers and inhabitants alike. Five hundred cases of smallpox were under treatment in the pesthouse at one time, which Greely had to visit twice a day, as commander of the hospital guard. Major Getchell of his regiment died in Greely's arms of yellow fever. Most of the servants ran away, so the officers had to care for one another.

But far worse than either of these diseases was the epidemic that followed, the dread Asiatic cholera, about which nothing was known except that you took it and died. In Greely's regiment, numbering eight hundred, 119 men died in one week. A man who was well at night would be found dead in the morning. One would be walking on sentry post and die a couple of hours later. It called for the greatest bravery, calmness and perseverance to maintain discipline and keep the commands intact.

During this period, our relations with France over her occupation of Mexico became very strained. Sheridan was ordered to Texas to form a corps of observation. Confederates and Federals alike would have rallied to the Union standard had war been declared against France, and the French, knowing this, rapidly withdrew their troops from Mexico.

While in Texas, Sheridan was quoted as saying, "If I owned hell and Texas, I would live in hell and rent out Texas." He denied that he had ever said it, but the story persisted. One enterprising Southern editor replied to it in these words: "Bully for Sheridan! Damn a man who won't stand up for his own country."

Greely had his first visit to Texas at this time also, when he was sent to Brownsville with some of his troops, in charge of a shipload of live stock for the army gathered in the lower Rio Grande valley.

When the volunteer army began to be discharged, Greely

41

was retained in service to assist in the organization of two new regular regiments, both colored. On his twenty-third birthday, March 27, 1867, he was mustered out of the volunteer army, after five years and nine months' service. A visit to Washington, where he presented military recommendations to Secretary of War Stanton, resulted in his being appointed as a second lieutenant in the 36th Regular Infantry. He thus became a professional soldier; the first one, he says, in many generations of his American ancestors. It has been the same with me. Although my ancestors always served in the military forces whenever their country was involved in war, they never remained as regular soldiers, except in my case, and it was Greely, then a General, who was responsible for that.

Shortly after he accepted his regular commission, Greely was ordered west, to Fort Sanders, Wyoming. At that time no railway reached beyond the Missouri River. The railhead was at Omaha, Nebraska. The Union Pacific was then being built to the westward, while the Central Pacific was working from the west toward the east. Construction of these roads through the hostile Indian country was a marvelous piece of work.

When Greely's train reached Plum Creek, Nebraska, it was held up by the report of an Indian attack. Moving forward cautiously, in a little while they came to a wrecked material train. The engine had been derailed by the Indians who had wounded and scalped the engineer, the rest of the train crew escaping. Something frightened the marauders off before they could burn the train, and they had even left the engineer's scalp behind, in their hurry. Greely saw it in a bucket of water in the caboose, where the wounded man was being cared for. Many years later he saw this man again, who had fully recovered although he was of course partly bald. He was still a conductor, and was very pleased to see some one who could corroborate his story, which he said people refused to believe at that time.

When the train came to the end of the operated track at Julesburg, Nebraska, they changed to stagecoaches. Due to danger of Indian raids, the coaches traveled in pairs, and every one, drivers and passengers alike, carried arms. They went through Denver, then a small hustling city, finally reaching Fort Sanders on the Laramie prairie, where besides the barracks and quarters there were several blockhouses, in which the garrison could defend itself against Indian attacks. This was no absurd precaution, as the 36th Infantry had been attacked by Indians the year before, in Dakota, with many casualties.

In the Indian country, Greely served protecting mail routes and convoys, and became thoroughly acquainted with those advance agents of our civilization. The West was being conquered with rapidity and Greely was one of the principal factors. As he expressed it, "There were Indians wild and peaceful, gold-seekers drunk and sober, stockmen smiling in rainy seasons and broken up in dry ones." There were soldiers, engineers, gamblers and camp followers. There were the pioneer women, so wonderfully courageous, who stuck with their men under conditions of hardship and privation not surpassed by the lot of primitive savages.

This part of Wyoming was then a hunter's paradise. Great herds of antelope and elk roamed the plains, plenty of bears were to be found in the hills, and the brush abounded in sage hens and other small game. Though the service was at times rigorous, marked by many discomforts, on the whole this outdoor life with its constant change of scene was a delightful existence for a young man of Greely's type.

He was next assigned to duty at Fort Douglas in Salt Lake City. The garrison had been put there to observe the Mormons, who had set up an independent government within our government, to handle things themselves. They ruled with an iron hand. At this time they were busy proselyting in Europe, especially in England, and many British joined them. Greely saw a great deal of the Mormon system and life, and came into intimate contact with the leaders of the church, including Brigham Young, whom he considered an extremely able organizer and administrator, with an acute understanding of individual men. He attributes most of the economic success of the Mormons to his ability. Under his leadership, they made a flourishing agricultural community out of this semi-arid region, by irrigating with water from the neighboring mountains; they built and maintained good roads; established business houses that handled not only the local trade, but that of the vast outlying region.

It seems to have impressed Greely greatly that the police force consisted of only one officer. Of this he afterward said: "Familiar with countless cities, domestic and foreign, I have never known another where life was so safe, property so secure, people so law-abiding and order so well kept as in Salt Lake City."

The Mormons referred to themselves as "saints," and to the outsiders, who then numbered only five percent of the population in Utah, as "Gentiles." The majority of the "Gentiles" were Jews, engaged in business. The army, government employees and overland stage force comprised the rest.

The principal amusements of the Mormons were dancing and theater going. The dances were held in the schoolhouse, and always opened by prayer. The Mormon Theatre was well attended, and boasted many first class attractions. Greely saw the mother of Maude Adams in a great many plays, and considered her theatrical talents fully equal to those of her daughter. In the pit of the theater, which was the "saint's" section, there were reserved two pews for the families of Brigham Young. A section of one bench had been cut out to provide space for the rocking chair that Brigham Young liked to sit in. Greely used to watch him from his seat in the gallery, and in the more than 50 performances that they both attended, he never saw Brigham smile, except at some humorous incident on the stage; nor did he pay the slightest attention to any of the women and children in his reserved section.

45

It was toward the end of 1867 that Greely was unexpectedly detailed to the Signal Corps, then the newest branch of the service, and it might be said that he and the Corps grew up together.

Chapter IV

JACK OF ALL TRADES

IT is of interest to note that the Signal Corps of the American Army was the first organization in any army devoted entirely to military signaling. Most of the other services had assigned this duty to their corps of engineers or to details from other branches of the service. While military signaling was used by all the great armies of antiquity, particularly the Romans, it was never brought to the state of perfection achieved by the American armies during the Civil War, when it was started as a separate corps.

Dr. A. J. Myer, a surgeon in the United States Army, had devised a signal code consisting of the numbers 1, 2, 3 with the signal flag. The "one" was a motion to the right, "two" to the left, and "three" straight ahead, for spacing or periods between words or sentences. A certain set system of changing these numerals to correspond with the letters, according to what was known as the cipher disk, was the secret method by which messages were transmitted during the Civil War. This code was used not only with flags in the daytime, but with torches and lamps at night.

The torch signalman was a picturesque figure. He wore waterproof and fireproof helmet, cape and gloves, because the burning kerosene continually fell on him. When he signaled at night, a small light was placed directly in front of him, another to the right and another to the left, so that his motions would be as nearly perfect as possible.

The distances at which these flag and torch signals were seen in the Civil War passes all credence. They were received through a 30-power telescope usually laid in sandbags and adjusted exactly on the sending station. Sometimes two or three observers watched for the signals simultaneously, which were called off and recorded by one of the men. It is a matter of record that with a four foot flag, signals were transmitted and received at the battle of Fredericksburg for a distance of 18 miles. There is no one living today proficient enough to duplicate this feat.

Signals were transmitted for comparatively short distances with a lamp, by jerking it in and out of a barrel, to indicate the numerals. The heliograph, an instrument which reflected the light of the sun, could flash messages, for thirty, forty or fifty miles, but as it depended upon sunlight, it could not always be relied upon.

Along with these went the field telegraph operated by the Signal Corps, which established for the first time in all history electric telegraph stations at the headquarters of armies and various corps during battle. It was the forerunner of the marvelous communications installed during the World War. Dr. Myer later became a general and head of the Signal Corps.

All line officers were taught something of signaling but the old line regular officers, steeped in conservatism, thought that

48

the best method of transmitting messages was by mounted couriers, and constant efforts had to be made to keep the Signal Corps from being disbanded.

When Greely was first detailed to the Signal Corps in 1867, he found himself the junior officer in the organization. Most of the other officers had graduated from West Point where they received an excellent literary and technical education. But Greely's great experience in war and the field, in every branch of the service, combining both theory and practice, and his superior mental attributes, made him stand out among his fellows. He was known as a jack of all trades. He was an excellent soldier, could learn things rapidly, had splendid command of men, was resourceful and could be depended on to finish any job given him. Electricity had interested him and he had studied a great deal about it.

At first he was given field duty as Signal Officer with the command of Gen. Eugene A. Carr, who in 1869 conducted a successful campaign in Nebraska against the Cheyenne tribe, under their chief, Tall Bull. The death of Tall Bull and the defeat of his followers at the Battle of Summit Springs ended active warfare for a time in this vicinity.

Then Greely was shifted to Wyoming, where at the Fort Laramie garrison the government was parleying with the dissatisfied Sioux, under the famous Red Cloud. A peace treaty was signed, giving the Indians the territory they wanted, and government troops were withdrawn from the forts in that area.

A second detail found Greely in Washington in 1870, when

the United States Weather Bureau was being established, and he devoted all his efforts toward the organization and development of this new branch of the Signal Corps. As the Signal system was the principal means of conveying information rapidly, it naturally followed that the Weather Bureau, whose reports had to be transmitted over the telegraph lines, should be assigned to the Signal Corps.

Systematic observations of meteorological conditions had been made in Europe for centuries but it was only in the nineteenth century, with the advent of telegraphy, that these efforts were concentrated, systematized and placed in the hands of specific bureaus by the various governments. Telegraph lines and submarine cables enabled weather data to be disseminated so rapidly that weather maps could be plotted and forecasts made from one to three days in advance.

At first the weather service was mainly for the benefit of shipping on the seacoast and the Great Lakes, but gradually it was extended to the interior of the country, and especially to the areas of the great rivers, whose annual floods wrought such havoc.

In 1872-73, Greely was detailed to gather data and formulate methods for the River and Flood Service. His researches caused the introduction of novel methods in the new River Division, for making earlier and more accurate flood forecasts. His work was so thorough and exact that today, after more than fifty years, the Flood Service pursues practically the same methods as then, having found no way in which radical improvements could be made.

This research formed the basis for the six pamphlets Greely wrote later on the climate of various portions of the Trans-Mississippi region. These were primarily for the benefit of prospective immigrants and settlers, to give them an idea of the conditions of rainfall and temperature they would encounter. Later, these documents proved of value in the development of irrigation and water power.

In 1875, bandit raiders from Mexico across the Rio Grande, combined with marauding Indians in the western part of Texas, caused Congress to make an appropriation for telegraph lines to be constructed along the frontier to more efficiently protect the settlers. Some ranking officers in the Signal Corps were detailed to construct these lines, but when a long time had elapsed with no results, Greely was called in by General Myer, then head of the Signal Corps, who told him to leave next day for Texas and finish the job.

Upon his arrival in Texas, Greely was told by his predecessor that it was practically impossible to construct the line as there was no timber for poles, the inhabitants were hard to handle, and the climate terribly hot. "Of course you will succeed," he added, with a smile, a remark that caused Greely to vow inwardly that he would accomplish what this other man found impossible.

He scoured the country for timber, but all he could get was some swamp oak, which was poor. Near San Antonio, the line was erected on scrub pine found in the nearby hills. The part from Fort Concho to El Paso, which crossed the treeless and waterless plains, was a difficult proposition. For this he found some timber in the mountains near Fort Davis and had it hauled down.

But the 400-mile stretch at the mouth of the Rio Grande was a hard nut to crack indeed, as there was not a single stick of timber in that vicinity. He finally located an old freighter who took a contract to deliver cedar poles from Fort Clark, but he would go no further than Laredo. This left 200 miles still unprovided for, and Greely was at his wit's end, until he remembered the Dismal Swamp in Virginia, where he thought he could obtain juniper poles. These were small and light and the freight would not be excessive. He was successful in this, making a contract for the delivery of poles at Point Isabel, near Brownsville, Texas, and the rest of the line was completed with poles brought 1,000 miles. By the end of the year he had constructed 1,100 miles of telegraph lines, which handled both military and commercial messages with as great precision as any telegraph company in the United States.

For a year Greely had worked and traveled an average of twenty hours daily, and consequently he was so worn out by these protracted and strenuous efforts that he was almost a wreck physically. He took a rest by going to Europe in 1876, where he learned a great deal about conditions and military and political systems.

He began the study of French, which he carried on to such good purpose that later he was able to conduct the meetings of the International Telegraph Conference in that language, when he attended its sessions in Europe.

In Marseilles he met the ex-Premier Adolphe Thiers, who had been the first President of the French Republic. Thiers was nearly eighty years old then. Greely records that he was "of tiny stature, not over-neatly dressed and unattractive to the eye," and his first impression of the famous man was disappointing. But later when he heard him speak to a crowd from the balcony of his house, he was stirred to great enthusiasm for his forcefulness, eloquence and vivacity. He read Thiers' "French Revolution" and his admiration was firmly established for this man who had struggled fifty years to promote the principles of personal liberty in his beloved country.

He spent some time in Paris, and made numerous friends in widely differentiated groups: the somewhat radical students, French politicians, military men and scientists. A distinguished acquaintance presented him to the fiery Gambetta one day, as he sat with some friends at a sidewalk café in the Latin Quarter. In this conversation, Gambetta displayed much interest in American affairs, questioning and commenting shrewdly on such things as the Custer massacre, news of which had just reached Paris, the size of the American army, the effects of the Civil War, the main differences between the Democrats and Republicans. Greely was won to him, and, probably from his partisan sympathies, declined an opportunity to meet Marshal MacMahon, then President of France, and Gambetta's political foe.

After six months of Europe, Greely regained his usual robust health and returned to the United States, where he was put on emergency duty again. This time it was to rebuild telegraph lines between Cape Hatteras, North Carolina, and Cape Henry, Virginia, which had been largely destroyed by a hurricane. Following this, in 1877, he was sent to the west to construct the line from Santa Fe, New Mexico, to San Diego, California, which he completed in six months.

It was during the construction of this line that Greely met the tall, dark-haired Henrietta Nesmith of San Diego, who was to be his wife. The Nesmiths came from an old family of New York, of Dutch extraction. During the winter and spring of 1861 they had been in the South and were caught there by the opening of the Civil War. They wandered about for a long time trying to get back North, eventually getting into Mexico and taking ship to New York from there. As soon as the transcontinental railroads were built, they moved to California.

Greely fell in love with the same thoroughness that he displayed in everything. Before six months had passed, he had courted and won the lovely Henrietta. They were married in 1878, at which time Greely was 34 years old. He stood six feet two and the young Mrs. Greely's height was five feet ten. His blue eyes and fair complexion were in pleasing contrast to her dark eyes and hair; his direct manner, rather puritanical attitude and exacting nature were complemented and assisted by her delicate tact and diplomacy. She was a woman of great social presence and ability, an adept at ironing out difficulties, and was to prove a wonderful helpmate to him all through their life together.

54

Upon his return to Washington, newly married, Greely was assured of continued duty in that city, but less than four months later he was ordered out to the frontier again. The annihilation of General Custer's command in 1876 by the Indians on the Little Big Horn had thrown the West into a turmoil. The Indian tribes were restless, often hostile, and terrified the scattered settlers. It was decided to build another telegraph line, from Bismarck, North Dakota, through to the Pacific coast. Greely had become what might be termed the shock officer of military communications. Wherever an emergency occurred, he was sent for, as he was the only one who knew every detail of frontier duty, whose knowledge of electricity and telegraphy was exact, and who had the energy necessary to push through such work.

It was quite a blow to the Greelys to give up their pleasant home in Washington, where they had expected to spend the first few years of their married life. But orders were orders, so they closed their house and Mrs. Greely accompanied her husband to the western frontier. There she became acquainted with the privations and make-shifts of pioneer life. First they lived in a boat on the headwaters of the Missouri River, then in a camp, then in various small settlements through which the line passed. She knew Indians, miners, settlers, freebooters, camp followers and the various types of hardy Americans who had surged to the West to develop the new country.

It is hard for us to realize today the difficulties encountered in the building of such a line, some 600 miles long. All

55

the equipment had to be transported by animals, through a country inhabited by hostile Indians, under harsh climatic conditions. Much of the country through which the line passed afforded no suitable timber and it had to be brought from hundreds of miles away, floated down connecting streams. At this time of the year, late summer, the water was very low and frequent sand-bars made it necessary to load and unload the logs many times on the trip. One crew mutinied and the ringleader assured Greely that those poles would never be used for a telegraph line, as they would be worn out loading and reloading.

By employing much ingenuity, Greely successfully carried out his orders, that "the lines must be in operation before the snow flies." Full of elation, he reported this from Deadwood, Dakota, to which point he had built the side line from Fort Keogh, and made ready for an immediate return to Washington. But to his dismay, he received a return wire, instructing him to inspect all the lines personally before leaving. Apparently it was not realized by his superiors what a rash and dangerous expedition this involved, a journey at the beginning of winter through the uninhabited Bad Lands, through Indian infested territory, with a furnished escort of only three men with a wagon.

Additional escort was promised him further on, at Powder River. There was nothing to do but start out, and two days later a violent blizzard struck them in the Bad Lands, which buried them in snow for thirty-six hours. The high wind made a fire impossible. When they finally emerged and made

56

their way to Powder River, a captain with a full troop of cavalry met them, looked at Greely curiously and inquired, "Where is the rest of your escort?" When Greely told him that was all the escort he had, he shouted, "What damn fool sent you into an Indian country with three men?" "A distinguished colonel of Civil War experience," answered Greely. "Well," said the captain, "you had nerve to come." "What else could a lieutenant do?" asked Greely. He decided then that the blizzard had been a blessing in disguise, as it had kept the Indians off the warpath.

He finished the inspection and got over the Missouri River on the last wagon that crossed it that winter, as it froze up the following day.

Chapter V

TO THE ARCTIC

ALL this service in the Signal Corps, his knowledge of electricity and instruments, and his familiarity with the work of the Weather Bureau, brought him in direct line for the command of the Arctic expedition of 1881-84, which turned out to be one of the most remarkable voyages into the unknown ever made by man. It was remarkable for the thoroughness of the arrangements made for the welfare of the party; the exactitude with which the duties of the expedition were carried out; the faithfulness unto death of those who passed away, and the grim tenacity of the handful left alive in their struggle to survive.

This expedition was no haphazard Pole-seeking adventure, promoted by private funds or for advertising or private gain. It was the result of an international agreement between several nations in the northern hemisphere to establish jointly a number of stations in the Arctic to report upon every phase of ice, water and climatic conditions, and to gather all information possible about the flora, fauna and geology of the region, thus giving the world a better realization of what the Arctic actually contained. It was the first time the United States as a government had acted in concert with other nations for a single purpose, which was the increase of human knowledge.

The expedition was authorized by Acts of Congress approved May 1, 1880, and March 3, 1881. It was to establish a station north of the 81st degree of north latitude, at Lady Franklin Bay, Grinnell Land, just across the Robeson Channel from northern Greenland. The force was to consist of volunteers, Greely and two other officers, twenty-one enlisted men and one contract surgeon, a total of twenty-five. Greely was authorized to spend the money appropriated to obtain necessary equipment and hire a steam whaler or sealer to transport the party from St. John's, Newfoundland, to Lady Franklin Bay. Minutely detailed instructions were given for the conduct of the expedition by General Hazen, then Chief Signal Officer. This order provided that a vessel should be sent them each year while they were in the Arctic. In case the vessel failed to reach them in 1882, she would cache supplies, letters and dispatches on the east coast of Grinnell Land, the same island on which the expedition was to be quartered, and also establish a small depot on Littleton Island, leaving notices of what had been done at Cape Hawks, Cape Sabine and Cape Isabella. It is important to remember this in view of what happened later.

The order further stated that in case the permanent station of Greely's command was not reached in 1882, that the vessel sent in 1883 would remain in Smith's Sound until danger of its closing by ice, and on leaving would land all her supplies and a party prepared for the winter's stay on

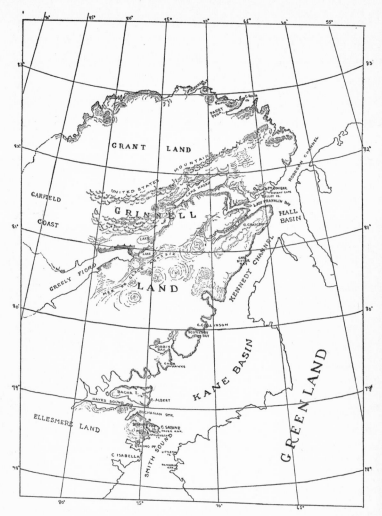

MAP OF THE PRINCIPAL GEOGRAPHICAL POINTS OF THE
GREELY EXPEDITION

Littleton Island, and send sleds up the east side of Grinnell Land to meet Greely's party. If not met in 1883, Greely was ordered to retreat to the south by the east coast of Grinnell Land.

Smith's Sound, north of Baffins Bay, was always thought to be an avenue of approach to the "Northwest passage" to the Pacific Ocean. In 1585, John Davis of Sandridge, England, sailed west and sighted Greenland, rediscovered as it were, because there was no record of Europeans having gone there since the Norse were extirpated from that country a couple of hundred years before. Davis sailed around the southern part of Greenland, beset by ice on all sides, and then coasted up along its Western side, where he found "many greene and pleasant Isles bordering upon the shore."

Another great seaman, William Baffin, followed in Davis' path in 1616. In a craft of only 55 tons, he sailed from England, went through Davis Strait and up as far north as what is now known as Baffin Bay. He reached a latitude of 77° 45′ north, which point remained as the "farthest north" for 236 years. His good fortune in getting that far was probably due to there being little ice during that year.

Various expeditions were made there in the nineteenth century. One of them records that the native Eskimos had knife blades and other implements made from meteoric iron which they found near Cape York. These indigenes knew nothing of any other people living further to the south.

This route, up through Davis Strait, Baffin Bay and Smith Sound, into Kane Basin, became a route for the explorers who followed, in their attempts to push north along the west coast of Greenland. In 1871, Capt. Hall in the ship *Polaris* succeeded in reaching the Polar Ocean on the last day of August. The object of this expedition was to reach the North Pole, but Captain Hall died, and the ship spent the winter at Thank God Harbor. Various parties were sent out from the ship, until in August, 1872, she was caught in the pack ice and carried steadily to the south. On October 15th, a violent gale almost destroyed the ship; the crew began landing stores upon the ice floe, and while thus engaged, the vessel broke away, leaving 19 men on the ice, including the captain of the ship. The floe drifted slowly south until eventually the party was picked up off the coast of Labrador by the sealer *Tigress* on April 30, 1873! These men had existed in the face of conditions under which it would not be thought possible to support life. On this cake of ice, for 196 days, 83 of which were without the sun, they had drifted over 1,500 miles. When they were picked up, they had of course given up all idea of ever being saved. The party who remained on the *Polaris* succeeded in beaching the sinking vessel at a place called Life Boat Cove, where they wintered. From the remains of the wreck they built two small boats in which they started for Upernivik. They were rescued, fortunately, on June 23, 1873, off Cape York.

Other expeditions, following along this same line, mapped the shores of Greenland and Ellesmere Island to the Arctic. These parties had the usual experiences of Arctic travelers, including deaths by frost bite, starvation and severe epidemics of scurvy. They had assembled a great deal of valuable information about meteorological conditions, climate and geography, which Greely studied closely. In the latter part of the nineteenth century, there was an even greater interest in fathoming the secrets of unknown regions than there is today, when the Poles not only have been reached over the ice, but have been flown over by aircraft.

The idea of the international circumpolar stations was conceived by Lieut. Charles Weyprecht of the Austrian Navy. He had been a member of an Arctic expedition which got stuck in the ice and drifted around for a long time, and discovered Franz Josef Land. When they were stuck in the ice a second year, Weyprecht abandoned his vessel and made his way by boats and sleds to Nova Zembla Island, where he was rescued by Russian fishermen. The drifting currents, the movements of the ice and the novel climatic conditions that were little known to the average scientist, impressed Weyprecht with the necessity of a systematic study of the Arctic. After a series of international conferences, it was decided upon.

While these conferences were going on, Captain Howgate of the United States Army, who was especially interested in the Arctic regions, sent the schooner *Florence* to the north in 1877, with a view of establishing an Arctic colony in Lady Franklin Bay. This was not successful, but Howgate succeeded in having Lady Franklin Bay designated as the point to be occupied by the United States Signal Service as its polar station, in connection with the international agreement.

Howgate helped push through the Act of Congress, approved May 1, 1880, which provided for the acceptance and fitting out of the steamship *Gulnare,* which he had purchased. Lieut. Greely was detailed for this service. The Navy Department, however, refused to acept the *Gulnare* for this work, which caused Greely to decline the command of the expedition. The ship proceeded north anyway but returned disabled, leaving Dr. Octave Pavy in Greenland.

Fourteen stations were eventually established, two by the United States, one at Point Barrow, Alaska, and the other at Lady Franklin Bay, in 81° 44' north latitude, the station farthest north. Observatories were established in lower latitudes to work with the polar stations, making the total number of observing stations over forty.

The Secretary of War was none too favorable toward this expedition, and the whole work of organizing and equipping it developed upon Greely, with an appropriation of $25,000. After many vessels were inspected, the steam barkentine rigged sealer, *Proteus,* of 467 tons, was selected. She was sheathed with ironwood from her waterline to below the turn of the bilge, her bow was armored with iron, and she was otherwise equipped for work in the ice. The captain and crew were entirely conversant with ice conditions in the Arctic. Three-fourths of the appropriation was required for chartering this boat, leaving only about $6,000 for the equipment of the party. This included scientific instruments, fuel, boats, dogs, fur clothing, food and camp equipage.

The personnel of the expedition was carefully selected

from many volunteers. Edward Israel, an astronomer and graduate of Ann Arbor University, enlisted in the army so as to accompany the expedition, as did Rice, a professional photographer. In addition to their technical and military training, most of the men had seen hard service on the western frontier, with its incidental dangers and exposure. Greely himself had long ago become inured to almost every physical hardship Nature had to offer, starting in at the tender age of 17 as a soldier in the Civil War, and taking in his stride all sorts of rough frontier duty and campaigns against the Indians.

His family in 1881 consisted of his wife and himself, and two little girls, Antoinette, aged three, and Adola, three months old. Instead of remaining in Washington, Mrs. Greely decided it would be better for her to go to San Diego, where her father's family still lived, and stay with them during her husband's absence in the Arctic. She knew it was to be a dangerous trip and possibly might turn into a desperate undertaking, but she gave her encouragement to him and his men, notwithstanding her natural fears.

The expedition assembled at St. John's, Newfoundland, in various detachments, traveling on commercial vessels. Here they took about a month in making their final preparations. On July 7, 1881, they left St. John's and headed for the north. Soon ice was encountered, then the bleak shores of the Arctic lands, shrouded by fog. A stop was made at Godhavn on the Island of Disco, an Eskimo settlement under Danish control. The houses here were of stone and turf, lined with wood, and the windows were made from seal intestines. There they bought a dog team of twelve animals, and a supply of dog food.

At Upernivik, the most northerly civilized settlement in the world, the expedition halted again. Upernivik means "spring" in the Eskimo language, but notwithstanding the fact that it was greener this year than in fourteen previous seasons, it seemed a desolate and barren spot.

Two Eskimos, Christiansen and Jens Edwards, were hired to accompany the expedition. All the skin and Arctic clothing possible was gathered from the Eskimos, and many birds, such as guillemots and small auks, were killed and added to the larder. Danish officials treated the expedition with the greatest courtesy. It was suspected that they charged high prices for what they sold but this was more than made up for by their hospitality with every form of wine and liquor available.

As the *Proteus* rounded Cape York, "pancake ice" was encountered which did not impede their progress, but a heavy fog held them up as they neared Smith Sound. So open was the water that they made the passage of the dreaded Melville Bay in only thirty-six hours, something quite unheard of. Their magnetic compasses began to give them trouble, as the variation from the true north increased vastly as they approached the Magnetic Pole.

Along the approaches to Smith's Sound were the remains of former expeditions in the form of stone cairns, some of which contained caches of food, about which Greely had information before he started. On the Cary Islands, Greely located and examined a depot of 3600 rations in fairly good condition, left by the Nares Expedition in 1875. Further on, at Littleton Island, some fifty cairns were found, only one of which contained any record. It was that the whaler *Eric* had touched there in 1876. After a diligent search, four boxes and three casks of mail matter were discovered, which had been landed in 1876 for the Nares expedition by Sir Alan Young.

Walruses were sighted for the first time near Littleton Island. They seemed unafraid of man, and those wounded showed a disposition to fight. White whales and narwhals were also seen, and a grampus pursuing whales and seals. There is a record of thirteen porpoises and fourteen seals being taken from the stomach of one of these voracious animals, which choked to death swallowing a fifteenth seal. Littleton Island seemed to be a favorite nesting place for eider ducks, thousands of which were seen.

As the *Proteus* pushed further north, Greely noted much unbroken harbor-ice in the bays, but few bergs were met with in Kane Sea. Entering Kennedy Channel, a northeast wind sent large fields of heavy ice directly across their way, and the *Proteus* had to dodge about to keep from getting stuck in it. Some of the floes were from one to five miles long, and ten to fifty feet thick. The captain, fearing a "beset-ment" (sticking in the ice) made arrangements for hoisting the ship's propeller and rudder, but before this was necessary, a favorable wind shifted the ice.

At 9 P.M. on August 4th, just five days after leaving Upernivik, the *Proteus* entered the extreme southeastern part of Lady Franklin Bay, a distance of about 700 miles. The ease and quickness of the voyage was unprecedented. In a measure this was unfortunate because it gave them unwarranted confidence, and this misleading conception of the usual difficulties to be encountered proved perilous to succeeding expeditions.

At Cape Baird, they were stopped by ice for the first time. A close heavy pack forced them to the south, and delayed them for several days, but on August 11th they reached their desired haven in Lady Franklin Bay, and a landing was made.

In order to approach the land closely, to facilitate landing the supplies, the *Proteus* began to break up the harbor ice, which averaged sixteen inches, but in places was eight or ten feet thick. The ship would back up several hundred yards from the edge of the ice, then go full speed ahead and strike the heavy floes with her iron bow. She would surge into the ice from a half to her whole length. As she moved forward, the crew rocked the vessel by running from one side to the other, so as to give a sideways motion, which helped break the floes and prevented the ship from being wedged in the ice. Under such circumstances, the commander of the ship needs to have had a great deal of experience to handle it skillfully, as the ship must be stopped and backed before entirely losing headway, to avoid wedging.

In addition to boats, Greely had provided the expedition

68

with a small steam launch, christened by Lieut. Lockwood the *Lady Greely*, in appreciation of the great interest Mrs. Greely had displayed in each member of the party. This was unloaded from the *Proteus*, together with a quantity of coal for fuel.

As the *Proteus* prepared to leave, three members of the expedition were sent back on her, as it was thought they were not well adapted to the service. One officer, Lieut. Kislingbury, who had not gotten on well with Greely from the first, was reproved by him during the six-day period when the ice-blocked ship was trying to get away, whereupon the lieutenant asked to be relieved and sent back to the United States on the *Proteus*. Greely consented and went ahead to put the order in writing, but this took just a little bit too long. While Kislingbury waited for the written order, the *Proteus* found a lead and broke through the ice. Kislingbury, going out over the ice toward her, saw her suddenly steaming away, and had to return to the station. Later he must have thought many times of the exceedingly narrow margin that had separated his chance for life and his ultimate terrible fate, death by slow starvation.

Chapter VI

LIFE AT FORT CONGER

THE *Proteus* at last disappeared, fighting her way through the ice, and the Greely expedition was alone, 250 miles north of the last Eskimo settlement, 1500 miles north of the Arctic Circle, and the most northern colony in the world, at 81° 44′ North Latitude.

A site was chosen for the camp, and construction of a house begun out of ready-cut lumber carried up on the *Proteus,* a new idea in 1881. The station was named Fort Conger after the United States Senator who had been so interested in the expedition. The house, consisting of three rooms, was 60′ x 17′, with double walls of half-inch boards, between which was an air space of about a foot to conserve the heat in the house. Covering the outside walls and roof and underneath the inside walls, were sheathings of tar paper. One room, 17 x 15 feet, was occupied by the officers, a larger room by the men, and the remaining space devoted to kitchen and bathroom. At both ends of the house were lean-tos of canvas and tar paper for storehouses.

Years later, in 1899, Commander Peary, discoverer of the North Pole, was making a sledge trip through this region and had his feet badly frozen, necessitating the amputation of eight toes. Finding Fort Conger in good shape, he spent sev-

Fort Conger, Grinnell Land, May 20, 1883

eral weeks there recovering. The following year he used it as a base for another dash north.

After the house was completed and the scientific instruments set up, a regular routine was adopted, including religious services on Sunday, and on week-day evenings lectures and addresses about various parts of the world, historical incidents and scientific matters.

The surface of the ground of Ellesmere Island, back of Fort Conger, was very rugged, with no timber of course. In summer and autumn it was swept free of snow in many places by the heavy winds. The elevations and ridges ran up from 3,000 to nearly 5,000 feet. For two or three months, in the summer, the temperature rose above freezing and streams poured down over the barren rocks from their glacial sources. Around the harbor the cliffs rose from 1,400 to 2,000 feet, almost straight up, and it was possible to get through them in only one or two places.

Shortly after the midnight sun in June the days rapidly shorten, the nights lengthen and the air becomes colder. In summer there are open stretches of water up into the Arctic Ocean, but as this begins to freeze and new ice is formed, it is very difficult to navigate, as the ice cuts into the sides of vessels not sheathed with metal or hardwood. Pressure on the ice is exerted by the constantly moving currents and tides in the Arctic Ocean. The ice field that results might be likened to Broadway in New York, if all the buildings on each side were made of ice and tumbled into the street, broken to pieces and up-ended. Travel across such a field is fraught with the greatest difficulty and danger. When the ice starts to freeze in the autumn, it is at first quite thin and a traveler attempting to cross it too soon will break through. On emerging, his clothing freezes instantly and if he cannot dry himself before a fire, the chances are he will be badly frostbitten or frozen to death. Only those who have lived in Arctic or sub-Arctic countries, and have done much traveling in the winter, can appreciate what it is.

The only fuel the Greely party had was what they brought with them, the fat from game they killed and some native coal. There was a seam of coal four miles from the camp which they could use on the steam launch and in their house, but of course they could not carry coal on the trail.

They had a small wheeled vehicle which they used wherever possible to carry supplies and cache them in various places for use in subsequent trips of discovery. The men often traveled carrying packs on their backs.

Caches left by former Arctic expeditions were found and their contents checked. In nearly all of them, a great proportion of the supplies were damaged as they had not been stored properly. They also found and identified the remains of other Arctic expeditions, consisting of sleds and other equipment. Whenever possible, members of the party hunted for game, such as musk-ox, seals, bears, dovekies and foxes.

In August the temperature had fallen considerably below freezing. The running brooks dried up, the yellow poppies wilted and the migratory birds began to go south. Only the saxifrage and daisies held on until September. It was not long before some of the men were frost-bitten. In the latter part of September, sledding was begun with dog teams, and determined attempts made to reconnoiter, discover and map all the land and water areas possible to reach.

Before total darkness set in, they had established four depots of food to the north, reconnoitered a good deal of country never visited before, put away three tons of fresh meat from their hunting, and gained a good idea of conditions at that time of the year. In that northern country, in addition to the animals and birds, there were a good many insects such as spiders, mosquitoes, flies, caterpillars, moths and daddy-long-legs, but the mosquitoes were not the terrible scourge they are further to the south in the Greenland ports. A few small fish were found in the fresh water lakes. From time to time the camp was approached by bands of wolves, one containing about eighteen animals. The dogs at the camp were terrified. Efforts were made to shoot or poison the wolves; a few were killed and the rest left the vicinity.

The sun disappeared on October 15th, but on October 25th one of the men came in with the astonishing information that the sun had come back! All rushed out to look, and there in the southern sky was a beautiful mock sun, a brilliant disk of blue, yellow and red, with bars of white light extending up and down. This extremely rare phenomenon lasted for almost an hour.

The expedition made hourly readings of the pressure of the atmosphere, temperature, dew point of the air, direction and force of the wind, quantity, kind and movement of the clouds, the aurora, and the state of the weather. Whenever possible the temperature of the water was taken, both near the surface and deep down, and notations made as to the thickness of the ice. Accurate readings were made of the declination of the magnetic compass needle. It is interesting to note that at Fort Conger in 1882, the magnetic needle pointed between west and southwest, the magnetic declination being 100° 13' west. The needle assumed almost a vertical position, the dip being about 85 degrees. Many of the observations made by this expedition were the first systematic ones carried out in the north. A large pendulum was installed with great care and used for time observations.

Samples of the air were taken from time to time, by filling and tightly corking bottles, with a view to having them analyzed to determine the oxygen content at various temperatures. Observations were made of the velocity of sound in cold temperatures. The number of observations made and recorded every day were: meteorological, 234; tidal, 28; magnetic, 264; a total of 526 every day. On certain days the number of magnetic observations made increased to over 1200. Each member of the expedition was detailed to do his proportion of the work, in accordance with his technical knowledge and ability.

Those who have not experienced the darkness of an Arctic winter, when the sun is gone for four and a half months, cannot appreciate the depressing effect this has on the spirit. The less one is occupied, the more this effect is felt. It undermines health, a man's face slowly acquiring a greenish yellow tint;

74

it makes the men's tempers bad, increases the difficulty in maintaining discipline, and sometimes leads to the breaking up of an expedition, especially if the commander is not an able man. There is a record of a party of Spitzbergen walrus hunters, all of whom perished from depression of spirits evidently, as they had an abundance of food on hand.

The Greely Expedition entered the winter of 1881 in excellent condition. The health of the men was carefully looked after, and preventive measures were taken against scurvy particularly. As a result, the expedition was remarkably free from this dreaded disease. Consideration was given to the effect on the men of dirt, dampness, excessive exercise or labor. A bath had been provided in the hut and all members were required to bathe at least once a week, and each Saturday a thorough cleaning took place.

In cold weather, men always have enormous appetites, as do animals and any living creature that has to exert itself. For two years, the daily ration used by the expedition consisted roughly of the following:

28 ounces of meat
10 " " vegetables (canned)
5 " " sugar
13½ " " farinaceous foods
5 " " canned fruits
3 " " dried fruits and pickles

or about 64 ounces of food in all. This was increased by coffee, tea, chocolate and condiments, 6 ounces, making a total of 70 ounces, which was entirely consumed. Canned tomatoes

75

were found to be the best vegetable, apples and peaches the best fruits. One hundred gallons of New England rum was on hand, which allowed each man 1½ gills weekly. The diet was varied and no one knew a day ahead of time what they were to have. Cooks were changed every month so as to afford a different style of cooking.

It seems to be generally accepted that Eskimos have enormous appetites, with a special predilection for seal blubber, but Greely records that while his two Eskimos ate heartily, their appetites did not surpass those of the other men, and they would not even taste seal blubber.

Men were assigned duty in the open air at least one hour a day, so as to give them sufficient exercise. Instruments were placed at some distance from the hut, so the men making the readings would have to take a walk. During the bright periods of the moon, ice was accumulated to be melted for drinking water. When the moon disappeared, this was practically impossible. The best ice was that of very ancient origin, known as palæocrystic ice, possibly thousands or millions of years old.

Greely had brought along a very good library, which proved to be a great source of interest and comfort during the dark months. Besides the scientific works, encyclopedias and books relating to the Arctic, there were over one thousand novels and magazines. Various games had also been brought, and a few musical instruments. Private Schneider, a young German, played the violin, his favorite selection being "Over the Garden Wall."

Sledding work was kept up to a certain extent during the dark period and coal was mined from the seam in Watercourse Ravine. At various places, houses were built of blocks of ice and equipped, probably for the first time, with coal stoves! After a month's experience in the darkness, expeditions were limited to one or two days, where comfortable shelters could be reached for the night.

It is thought by many that the nearer one is to the North Pole, the brighter and more frequent are the displays of the aurora borealis, but this is not the case. There is a belt at 60° north latitude where they are most frequent, some thousand miles south of where Greely's expedition was quartered. However, they often saw the aurora.

On November 8th, the last sledding party returned. The mean temperature for the month was 24° below zero. As the darkness increased, the depressed spirits of the men were very marked, but especially the two Eskimos, one of whom wandered off in a semi-dazed condition, until rescued by members of the expedition and brought back. It is a strange fact that after the shortest day of the year, December 21st, was passed and the sun began its northern journey, although visual evidence of a change was not perceived by any one, the spirits of the men were greatly improved.

Christmas was celebrated in a fitting manner. In preparation for the holiday, the floors and walls of the house were thoroughly washed, as much soot and dirt had accumulated on them. That may sound like an ordinary incident but it was really quite a task, as the water froze on the walls and floors continuously and the ice had then to be scraped off. Afterward, Sergeants Brainard and Rice decorated the rooms with flags, pennants and anything else that could be draped about. On Christmas Eve, the hut presented a bright and cheery appearance. All the presents were spread out on the table, as no Christmas trees grew in this Arctic zone. Due to the forethought of Greely, there were gifts for every one, wrapped and addressed to each person individually. It is little incidents like his thought of Christmas presents that gives one an insight into the true nature of the man. Brainard writes of him: "... a silent and often taciturn man, his tender heart and unfailing fairness won for him the affection and the loyalty of his command under very difficult circumstances."

Christmas Day, which came on Sunday that year, was clear and cold, and everybody took a walk along the ice-foot. The Psalms for Christmas were read in the morning, followed by a hymn and the doxology led by Lieut. Kislingbury. Greely says that he remembers but one other service in the Arctic, their first burial, that so affected and impressed the men.

Sgt. Frederick, the cook on duty at this time, had devoted several days to preparing a fine Christmas dinner on their big cooking range. The menu was as follows: Mock-turtle soup, salmon, fricasseed guillemot, spiced musk-ox tongue, crab-salad, roast beef, eider ducks, tenderloin of musk-ox, potatoes, asparagus, green corn, green peas, cocoanut pie, jelly cake, plum pudding with wine sauce, ice cream, grapes,

78

cherries, pineapples, dates, figs, nuts, candies, coffee, chocolate! Eggnog, rum and cigars were handed around later.

On January 16th, they were visited by a violent storm, which in one respect was extraordinary. The general principle is that such storms do not occur at low temperatures. About 10 A.M., in a sub-zero temperature, the barometer commenced falling rapidly, hour by hour; the air was full of snow and the wind increased in force until at 13 below zero it was blowing at 52 miles an hour, an unparalleled occurrence in Arctic records; an hour later it was 62 miles, then 65, finally changing to violent gusts that attained a velocity of 80 or 90 miles an hour. The high, screaming note of the wind, the creaks and groans of the house as it shook and shivered under the blasts, made them fear the roof would be twisted off and the whole structure blow away; but it held staunchly, and after some five or six hours of suspense, the wind dropped suddenly and finally died away.

The coldest day of the winter was in February, around 60 below zero. Two Arctic hares were shot during the month, one of which weighed eleven pounds. As February wore on, light began to return and the southern sky reflected the most glorious colors; sometimes a deep, rich red, shading into purple, sometimes a medley of colors from a gold bar on the horizon, through Nile-green to a clear bright blue directly overhead, the northern sky an intense midnight blue.

On one of these days an expedition set out to read the instruments on Bellot Island, and returned some five hours later in good shape but complaining of many falls on the ice, as without shadows it is extremely difficult to note the inequalities of the ground.

All during the month, equipment was gotten together and careful preparations made for sled journeys. On February 28th, the sun appeared for the first time. In the early part of March, sledding parties started out, using the system of establishing caches followed by most Arctic explorers and others crossing areas where no supplies are available. Sleds are sent out heavily loaded and deposit what they have left at the end of their specified journey, then return to the starting point. The next ones go a little further and deposit their load. When sufficient supplies have been accumulated far enough away to enable the actual explorers to get to the place desired, as few men and dogs as possible to attain the objective are sent, so as to use the least amount of supplies.

Greely gives an interesting description of how they camped while traveling in temperatures of 30 and 40 below zero:

"An order to camp is obeyed with alacrity, not that it is a comfortable or pleasant thing to do, but because work of any character is preferable to standing quietly around. The only continued comfort for an Arctic sledger is while he is engaged in the drag ropes hauling a fair load at a moderate pace over a level bit of ice.

"With skilled hands the sledge is rapidly unlashed, and while the main party sets up the tent the evening cook is searching out a blue-topped berg, from which to get his ice for tea and stew. The tent is well pitched on a proper site, which preferably is a level snow-covered bit of floe, with a large berg near to the windward to break the force of any sudden gale. If snow cannot be found suited for the site of the tent, it is best that snow be brought and strewed within it. This not only gives a soft bed, but a comparatively warm one, for ice is invariably colder than snow.

"The rubber tent-cloth spread, the sleeping bags are brought in and laid down, but to unroll them is a labor demanding the strength of a Hercules. The moisture which exhaled the night before from the body, the falling spiculae of snow formed that morning in the tent, the lingering vapor from the stew and the drops of spilled tea have all insidiously worked their way deep into the tangled hair, and turning to ice, have bound fast the tightly rolled buffalo bags. Now they are more like coils of rolled sheet-iron than the supple well-tanned skins they are supposed to be. By great exertions they are finally forced apart, and the wise sledge traveler seeks them at the earliest moment.

"The work of erecting the tent and opening the bags has necessitated the use of the bare hands in a measure, and handling these articles, colder than frozen mercury, is like handling hot iron which burns and cracks men's fingers and hands. The comparatively light work, too, has checked the perspiration, and with stiffening clothing and half-frozen fingers the travelers, other than the cook and commissary sergeant, sit down; and carefully brushing the snow from their garments, loosen the lashings and take off overalls and footgear. They arrange these in the shape in which they can easiest don them, for in five minutes after they are frozen solid. The feet are stripped bare and a pair of fresh socks, warm from the man's breast, are put on and covered at once with a pair of large dogskin or sheepskin sleeping socks. Crawling into the bag, their chilled limbs gradually thaw out the frozen skin and later they acquire warmth when hot tea and stew come to them.

"The cook meanwhile has obtained his ice, both for morning and evening meal, and has received from the sergeant the carefully measured allowance of alcohol. His ice cut too coarsely or mixed with too much snow, and the wicks half an inch too high or too low, and the result is a stew mixed with ice, or tea just steaming and uncooked.

"The rations, arranged at the station, are served out with the same careful exactness. An ounce too much today means shortage tomorrow. The cooking apparatus carefully placed level on a board, he watches it with the utmost caution, for the arrangement is such that carelessness, or perhaps the sudden movement of a man in the bag, may cause a pot to tip and the precious allowance to be lost. An hour is a moderate time in which to cook the tea, and as the frozen wretched cook watches it he realizes too keenly the truth of the adage, 'A watched pot never boils.'

"The pot finally boils, and instantly it is served to the weary men, some of whom, overcome by the exhausting labors of the day, have dropped off into a sleep and are doubtful whether to be vexed or pleased that they are recalled to a sense of cold and weariness. The steaming tea and stew are served, the clouds of vapor change to falling snow; the weary men, refreshed by their meal, crawl down in their bags, to be followed by the cook as soon as he can arrange his lamp and pot and tie up the tent securely.

"The night, or rather the hours set for sleep, passes slowly. Crowded two or three into one bag, all must be awakened and turn together whenever cramp or cold renders one so uncomfortable that he must change his position. Stiffness, aches, rheumatic pains, cold and cramps fall to every one's lot. Nobody is sorry, save the cook, when the officer calls that unfortunate person, whose only comfort is the reflection that his service passes with that meal, as the cooking is done in turn.

"In the morning the same routine is gone through with, modified at times by some depraved article of footgear, which, frozen into metal-like hardness, will not be coaxed or forced on to the foot until it has been taken literally to one's heart and thawed out by the heat of the body. The slowness with which the party breaks camp makes everybody wretched and ill-humored until a short march has thawed traveling gear and human nature into tractable mood.

"With the temperature 75 degrees or more below the freezing point of water, it seems to me surprising even now that men can ever do and endure such work and exposure. Only those of perfect health, iron constitution and marked determination are capable of continued work under such conditions. This account of a camp is a fair description (underdrawn if anything) of the experiences of a sledging party favored by fine weather and ordinary travel. When storm and snow come to blind, wet and buffet the travelers, their miseries cannot be described in words. Such conditions as above must be imagined as the common experience of all Arctic travelers until zero temperatures come with May, bringing other discomforts not much less serious."

Chapter VII

GREELY himself explored the interior of Grinnell Land and Grant Land in April and May, and found there great fresh water lakes, with willows and grass growing, which furnished abundant subsistence for musk oxen, and certainly at one time reindeer, although none of the latter was seen. Many kinds of birds were found, including geese, ducks, ptarmigans, falcons, owls, eagles, plover, phalaropes, snow buntings and other small species. Fish of the salmon family were in the lakes. They found many former abodes of Eskimos, including interesting relics of whalebone, walrus ivory, wood and iron. These people apparently have gone as far north as any land exists not covered by an ice cap and have maintained themselves through the Arctic winters. This area in interior Grinnell Land is entirely free from an ice cap. It abounds in flowers and grasses and running streams of water in the summer.

From Greely's explorations, the United States had a claim to this land by right of discovery, but unfortunately when the Virgin Islands were bought from Denmark, our rights in this area were ceded to that country. Had the advice of any airman been sought when this transaction was taking place, decided recommendations would have been made against giving up this land which would form an ideal air base for commercial air traffic to Europe and Asia, or in case of war. In 1920, I wished to send an aerial expedition to that locality to show its great future utility.

An expedition sent out on April 3rd, under Lieut. Lockwood, with Sgt. Brainard as assistant and Christiansen as dog driver, proceeded north from Lady Franklin Bay along the coast of Grinnell Land, across the Robeson Channel to northern Greenland, and on May 13, 1882, established the "farthest north" which any one had attained up to that time, latitude 83° 24' N., longitude 40° 46' W. The farthest north record had been held for over three centuries by Great Britain. This accomplishment of Lockwood and Brainard, definitely established by adequate astronomical observations which have never been questioned, was received with intense interest by the scientific world when it was published two years later. Years afterward, Peary, in one of his expeditions toward the North Pole, visited this camp and secured the report, which he is said to have brought back to the United States.

After determining that they had reached the farthest north, Lockwood and Brainard built a large conspicuous cairn at Lockwood Island, about 30 feet above the level of the ice foot, in which they deposited a record of the journey. They scaled the hill behind the beach and unfurled the American flag which Mrs. Greely had presented to the expedition.

Great difficulties and privations were encountered on the

trip. On the way back, the dogs, which could be fed only every other day, became ravenous and started stealing the men's rations, so that they had to pack them more securely and hide them away. After they met the supporting party, a wind storm struck their camp, so violent that the men were frequently blown down, and a heavy sledge, with a 200-pound load, was lifted bodily from the ground, striking Ralston in the forehead and severely injuring him. At another place, huge rocks rained down on them from the cliffs above, forcing them to seek a new and more circuitous route. Rough ice wore out their sledges. On April 20th, the temperature fell to 40 below zero, very low for that date. Gales blew snow in their faces with such force that it was like a giant pelting them with gravel with all his strength.

The whole party returned to Fort Conger successfully, after a 60 days' absence, all well except two, who had become snowblind. This occurred during a dark day when they thought it unnecessary to wear their snow glasses.

On this trip they traversed 1075 miles, not only establishing a farthest north record, but adding 125 miles to the map of the Greenland coast.

Greely discounted the probability of a vessel reaching them that year and continually sent out parties to kill musk ox, geese or other game. Musk meat formed the principal item of their diet. During the latter part of the summer, the musk ox averaged 377 pounds dressed, whereas in June, before the grass and vegetation was green, they averaged only 200 pounds.

The party even attempted a garden, planting lettuce, cabbage and radishes, but it was not successful, probably owing to the alkalies in the soil. Greely stored the unused seeds in their hermetically sealed glass jars in the attic at Fort Conger, where they stayed, exposed to a temperature of 60 to 70 below zero, until 1899, when Dr. Dietrich, attached to Peary's Expedition, found them and took them back to the United States with him. He kept them five years, and at the request of the seed company that had supplied them, planted some of them. The radish, he found, grew 50 percent, and it was all of 23 years old. It is about the longest lived of all seeds, but hitherto it was thought to be good for only eight or nine years.

During their expeditions, the men found fossils of various kinds, some of which contained specimens of coral, showing that at one time tropical conditions prevailed there. Sergeant Brainard discovered a petrified forest with big trees.

Trips were made to various headlands during the latter part of the summer to gain what information they could about a possible relief vessel. A ship had, in fact, been sent north to their relief. General Hazen, the Chief Signal Officer, had been busy during the winter obtaining appropriations from Congress for the additional supplies to be sent north. Our consul in St. John's, Mr. Molloy, was ordered to purchase suitable supplies locally. The governor of North Greenland was asked to provide sealskin pants, sleeping bags lined with dogskin, leather thongs for traces and lines, sledges and personal equipment for the men while traveling over the ice.

William M. Beebe, Jr., General Hazen's secretary, was selected to take charge of the relief expedition of eight soldiers and a surgeon. He had served through the Civil War, entering as a private and attaining the volunteer rank of Major. A naval officer, Commander S. D. Greene, sent to St. John's to inspect a suitable vessel to be chartered for the expedition, reported that the steam sealer *Neptune* offered the most favorable terms, so she was chartered, loaded, and the First Relief Expedition left St. John's on July 8, 1882.

Beebe's orders were to proceed to Lady Franklin Bay in Grinnell Land and report to Lieut. Greely for orders. If unable to reach his destination, he was to establish depots "A" and "B" requested by Greely in a memorandum sent back the year before by the *Proteus*. It was made plain that these depots should not be established if it were at all possible to get to Lady Franklin Bay. Depot "A" was to be made at a prominent point on the east coast of Grinnell Land, the same island on which Greely's party was situated, and just as far north as possible. Besides the regular supplies for this depot, there were a whaleboat and a large quantity of mail matter, also sledges and twenty or thirty dogs. Depot "B" was to be placed on Littleton Island. All packages and cases were marked and stowed in a proper manner on the ship for these depots. Explicit instructions had been issued for the manner of making caches, wood and canvas being provided for se-

curing them. Records of these caches and directions for finding them were to be left at suitable places.

Soon after leaving St. John's, the *Neptune* began to encounter ice. It must be remembered that the ice conditions
of the previous year when the Greely Expedition went to the
Arctic were remarkable for the small amount of ice present.
This made it seem to subsequent expeditions that the trip
would be easier than it actually was, and they discounted
the possible dangers.

As she pushed north, the *Neptune* met more formidable
ice, and a succession of gales that caused her to lose an
anchor, besides other mishaps. On August 9th, the ship was
beset and helpless in the pack, twelve miles from Victoria
Head. She drifted northward for a couple of days, then on
the 11th the pack again closed in on her, piling up broken
fragments of ice as high as the bulwarks. On August 15th,
the ice released them and open water was reached. On the
18th they made Payer Harbor, adjacent to Cape Sabine, not
quite 200 miles south of Lady Franklin Bay. They tried to
work their way north through the heavy pack ice but were
unsuccessful and turned back. A gale came up from the
southwest and the captain of the *Neptune* insisted on going
to Pandora Harbor on the Greenland side for anchorage,
where they stayed until August 25th.

Another effort was made to reach Grinnell Land but the
ice pack checked them. On August 27th, after more or less
feeble attempts to break through, they returned to Littleton
Island on the Greenland side, where they saw a party of

Eskimos. They were afraid to land supplies while these people were about, as they might appropriate them, therefore they set out again for Grinnell Land, and succeeded in reaching Cape Sabine on August 31st, where they made a cache. This was the northernmost point they attained. They were again hit by gales, after which they made another futile attempt to push north. Being repulsed, they turned back and established a cache on Littleton Island. On September 5th, they decided to return south, and reached St. John's on September 24th.

Although provided with dogs and sledges and sufficient equipment to have landed a party and pushed north along Grinnell Land to Greely, no serious attempt was made to do it. The idea uppermost in their minds seems to have been to save themselves; so Greely was abandoned to another year without help from the United States.

As the days shortened and the long dark winter approached without a ship having come, things began to seem a bit gloomy. However, there was plenty of food on hand with slight restrictions to last until the next summer, as everything had been handled very carefully. The spirits of the men were excellent. There had been no death or serious accident in the party. The only breach of discipline that had occurred was when Cross, the engineer, got drunk on fuel alcohol stolen while on a launch trip. He fell overboard and was rescued by Brainard.

In January, Greely was already making plans for a move, in case no relief reached them during the next summer. It was decided that if a ship had not appeared by August 8th, they would make their way south to Cape Sabine, in boats, and if possible cross over from there to the Greenland coast. On the last day of January, when the temperature was 40 or 45 below zero, they began carrying supplies to Cape Baird, 12 miles away, on the southern side of Lady Franklin Bay, it being easier to load the boats at Cape Baird than at Fort Conger.

The winter passed, and the men were found to be in even better health than the year before. Better arrangements were made for the spring trips, and new sleds were built on an improved pattern. Some of the sledge dogs had given birth to twelve stalwart puppies, which were carefully raised and trained by Schneider. They were now old enough to work. The dogs averaged seventy pounds in weight and the loads assigned them were 150% of their own weight, something over 100 pounds apiece. With these heavy loads, they traveled about three miles an hour, or with light loads about six miles, an excellent average in the Arctic.

Lieut. Lockwood was sent out in the same direction he had taken the year before and accomplished in six days what it had previously required 22 days to do; but he struck open water and could not cross to Greenland. Had he not been stopped thus, he could unquestionably have gone a good deal further north than the year before. At one time he and his dog teams were nearly carried away to the Polar Sea on an ice floe, when the pack ice broke off suddenly. Fortunately they found a place where the ice had jammed temporarily and by quick work were able to reach land over this, with their dogs and baggage, before it too broke away from shore.

Less than two weeks after their return, Lockwood, Brainard and Christiansen started out again, this time in an effort to cross Grinnell Land from east to west and reach the "Western Ocean" as it was called then. The year before a party had been turned back in this attempt, but this year they made it. Besides other valuable discoveries, they reported the great Mer de Glace Agassiz, a glacier that extends across Grinnell Land for 85 miles like a Chinese Wall. It has a perpendicular front from 125 to 200 feet high and forms, with the glacial ice cap of the United States Mountains, the southern boundary of the extraordinarily fertile belt of Grinnell Land.

Greely had a right to be satisfied with the work of the expedition. They had circumscribed one-eighth of the globe above the 80th parallel, and explored and mapped thousands of miles of unknown territory.

All the records and equipment of the expedition were carefully packed. Most of the men turned in their diaries which were sealed, addressed and placed in watertight boxes. Every one realized that the journey on which they were to embark was a perilous undertaking. Their shortage of provisions and the impossibility of getting sufficient game during the ensuing winter at Fort Conger would have made the move necessary even if their orders had not required them to do so.

The ice in Kennedy Channel broke up on July 24th and

in Discovery Harbor on July 30th. August 8th arrived, the day for the retreat, and no boat had appeared. Conditions for the departure were unfavorable, the water not being open enough; but on the 9th the men boarded the boats and Fort Conger was abandonded. At Greely's command, several barrels of seal blubber, pork, beef and bread were opened so the dogs could get at them and maintain their lives for several months. These faithful animals could not be taken along, but if the expedition was forced back there, the dogs could again be utilized.

They took with them 50 pounds of duplicate records, the originals together with the natural history specimens being left in strong boxes at Fort Conger; also they carried their pendulum, which with its case weighed 100 pounds. The men were restricted to 8 pounds of baggage, the officers to 16 pounds. They abandoned enough salt meats, hardtack, coffee, tea and other articles for a scant year's army ration, not enough for an Arctic ration. Their flour, sugar, vegetables, milk and butter were either all gone or only scant quantities remained.

At this point, Greely makes the following entry in his diary:

"We then knew not that one relief steamer was at the bottom of the sea, and that its consort, its commander 'convinced that this frozen region is not to be trifled with,' was that very day steaming safely southward, with undiminished stores, into the harbor of Upernivik. And so we turned homeward, knowing we had the courage to face the blinding gale, the heavy floes, the grinding pack, the countless other dangers which environ the Arctic navigator; and having also, though we knew it not, heart and courage to encounter uncomplainingly, on barren crags, the hardships and horrors of an Arctic winter, with scant food, shelter and clothing, with neither fires, light nor warmth, and to face undauntedly intense cold and bitter frost, disaster and slow starvation, insanity and death."

Chapter VIII

THE RETREAT TO SABINE

THE expedition then began a series of Arctic water experiences that would try the bravest heart. Lieut. Greely went in the launch with eight others, the remaining sixteen being distributed in the three boats which the launch towed. Forty full rations for each man were carried. It was known that there were some caches of provisions further south.

They encountered blinding gales, drenching rain and snow, dense fogs, heavy ice floes and grinding packs. At one place they were met by a solid wall of ice, fifty or sixty feet high, which blocked the channel. They found a crack in this floeberg, 100 yards long but barely wide enough to let the launch go through with its tow. It looked as though at any moment it might close up and crush them, but they got through unscathed.

Cross, the engineer, again tampered with the fuel alcohol, and while under its influence, allowed the launch to ground on the bow, so that two hours were lost freeing her. A few days later he got drunk again, becoming quite insubordinate and refusing to obey orders. Everything went wrong in the engine room and Greely had to put another man in charge. Tides were very heavy at this point, ebbing an inch a minute, so strict watch had to be kept. If the launch grounded, it was

95

a serious matter as thus they might lose a chance at following a lead through the ice.

All down the coast they picked up the different caches of which they had knowledge. At Cape Craycroft, they got 100 pounds of meat and a barrel of bread; at Carl Ritter Bay, the small cache landed in 1881 from the *Proteus,* 200 rations; at Cape Collinson, the Nares cache of 1875, 240 rations consisting of meat, salt, pepper, onion powder and fuel. The tobacco, sugar, tea and rum were missing. At Cape Hawks, the northernmost of three points where the relief party had been directed to leave word or make a cache, they hoped eagerly to find some news; but no one had stopped there for them. They secured the old English cache left years before, but found most of the bread spoiled; the remainder consisted of 168 pounds of dried potatoes, 342 pounds stearine, 6 gallons of rum and a keg of pickled onions. The bread barrels and casks were broken up and used for fuel on the launch as they had only one-fifth of a ton of coal remaining. On this fuel it was thought they could get to Littleton Island where there was a coal cache.

The ration issued now was a pound of meat and a pound of bread daily; beans or potatoes, two ounces; tea or coffee; and an occasional issue of fruits, such as apples or cranberries. Christiansen shot a seal and the hungry men found that its blood was quite palatable; Greely records that it tasted something like white of egg.

After Cape Hawks, they steered for Bache Island; but on August 26th, they were beset in the ice. New ice formed constantly and in a day or two was thick enough to bear the weight of a man. For fifteen days they remained stuck fast, drifting slowly southward with the pack for 22 miles. Several times the launch was nipped, being lifted bodily out of the ice, but it held staunchly. The small boats were drawn up on the floe. It was evident by this time that their only chance of escaping the pack was for a gale to come up and clear a path for them through the ice of Kane Basin; but the weather continued ominously calm, with a steadily falling temperature.

When about twelve miles from Cocked Hat Island, they decided that if they were to make land, now was their best chance; so the launch was abandoned, the equipment repacked and put on newly constructed sledges, which, with one of the boats, they pulled along over the ice. At this time, and later, Greely offered to abandon the heavy pendulum; but as the value of their Arctic observations depended upon subsequent comparative observations made with this same pendulum, and the men knew this, they would not hear of giving it up.

About a mile a day was made on the ice pack, but as a violent gale came up, the pack was moved from one place to another, losing the mileage they had gained in their drift southward. They were camped on a huge floeberg, at the mercy of winds, currents, temperature and tides; yet notwithstanding their perilous position, and the difficult conditions of life, their spirits remained high. Comfortable sleep or rest was out of the question, and the proper preparation of food all but impossible; yet they sang songs and danced on the ice.

Under these hard circumstances, the remarkable maintenance of discipline reflects great credit on the commanding officer. It is true that at times there was some insubordination, especially in the case of Lieut. Kislingbury and Dr. Pavy. The doctor was of French extraction, from New Orleans, and had always pursued a bohemian mode of life. He had a nervous, excitable disposition, was impatient of restrictions and in times of hardship and strain his moral fiber was apt to break down. However, as a physician and surgeon he was able and resourceful; keenly intelligent, well educated, observant, socially graceful, he was a pleasant and stimulating companion when things were going well.

When the launch was first beset in the ice, Greely had favored abandoning her at once, placing the party on a floe and drifting southward. His views were not approved generally. Lieut. Kislingbury, Dr. Pavy and Sergeant Rice approached Brainard with a proposition that shocked him, namely that Dr. Pavy should give a medical opinion that Greely was too ill to remain as the leader and Lieut. Kislingbury should supplant him. Of course Brainard refused in no uncertain way to join in this scheme. He records as his opinion that the chief actors never gave up the idea. It will be remembered that Lieut. Kislingbury had been suspended from exercising command in the party, and was treated merely as one attached for rations. Dr. Pavy undoubtedly influenced Kislingbury to take this action.

Scouting parties were sent out from time to time to discover the best route for reaching land. On September 16th, when their floe was 19 miles from Cape Sabine and 30 miles from Cairn Point, on the Greenland coast, Greely considered they should make an effort to reach Greenland. He reasoned that at Cape Sabine their troubles only commenced as it would be impossible to cross the straits there by boat or sledge, with the Arctic night upon them; while if they could make Greenland, bearing in mind the caches on Littleton and Carey Islands, their future would be assured.

Day by day, toiling strenuously, they moved their provisions from floe to floe, across open lanes of water, often finding after hours of work that they were further from shore than when they started, owing to the drift and wind. All the time in their ears was the portentous roar of the grinding pack to the east, in the axis of the channel. A violent storm set in on September 25th, which drove the floes decidedly toward the other shore, so they abandoned their efforts to reach Greenland. By this time, all of the party were verging on exhaustion and most of them were ill of diarrhea, caused by eating too much fresh meat—almost every day a harbor seal had been shot. During this storm, their floe cracked in two, just at the point where they had built a snow house and the men barely escaped onto a larger piece with their equipment. 55507

All through these trying times diaries were correctly kept and scientific observations made. At last, on September 29th, the floe was forced toward the shore, where it lodged against a grounded iceberg, and a landing was made at 5:20 P.M. It was 34 days since they had first been beset, and 19 days that they had been drifting on the ice, during which time they had only made 11 miles. They were lucky not to have drifted into Baffin Bay, where they undoubtedly would have been lost.

The place where they landed proved to be Eskimo Point, about 20 miles south of Cape Sabine. It had taken them 51 days to reach this place from Fort Conger, and they had traveled 500 miles to make 200. The whole party was in a healthy condition, although tired, and all the scientific papers, instruments, baggage, arms and ammunition were landed safely.

Walruses appeared here and every effort was made to kill them, some being shot but not secured. If a few walruses could be taken, their existence through the winter would be made certain, but here luck was against them again.

Upon taking stock of their rations, it was found that they only had 35 days' food, but they knew that an English cache of 240 rations was at Cape Sabine. It was decided to make the 35 days' rations last 45 days. A site was selected and work begun on three huts, the old Eskimo habitations there furnishing plenty of stones.

They now considered that they had three chances for their lives: first, finding an American cache from a relief vessel at Cape Sabine or Cape Isabella; second, of crossing the straits to the Greenland side when they froze over and reaching the

Eskimo settlement at Etah; third, of killing sufficient walruses and seals to last them during the winter.

October 7th was Mrs. Greely's birthday and it made the commanding officer reflect on how his wife and children would feel if the expedition should perish, as did Franklin's.

Upon volunteering, Sgt. Rice, the photographer, an exceptionally energetic and resourceful man, was sent to Cape Sabine with Jens, the Eskimo, to see if any cache had been left there. He returned on the 9th and reported a cache of 1300 rations (which proved to be incorrect) placed there from the *Proteus* on July 24th. A note left by Lieut. Garlington, U. S. Army, commanding the relief expedition, stated that the *Proteus* had been nipped on July 23, 1883, had been exposed to enormous pressure and had finally sunk. There was not sufficient time to save many of the provisions. What rations could be gotten hold of, some sleeping bags, tea and canned goods were landed and cached in a hurry, and no marker was left. The note also stated that all were saved from the *Proteus,* and that the U.S.S. *Yantic* was on her way to Littleton Island, with orders not to enter the ice. Everything within the power of man would be done to rescue them, wrote Garlington. The party took this to mean that further efforts would be made to reach them at once, so Greely decided to proceed to Cape Sabine and await the promised help.

Chapter IX

WRECK OF THE SECOND RELIEF EXPEDITION

LET us turn now for a moment to the Relief Expedition sent north under Lieut. Garlington. On account of the failure of the Beebe expedition to reach Greely, efforts were redoubled to accomplish this the following year. Lieut. E. A. Garlington, 7th Cavalry, was chosen from volunteers as the commander. A year's supplies of food and clothing, arms, ammunition, dogs, sledges, boats and other equipment were assembled at St. John's, also a year's provisions for the crew of the steam sealer *Proteus,* the same vessel that had transported Greely's party. The naval vessel *Yantic* was sent to accompany the *Proteus,* to act as a tender. The *Yantic* had not been constructed specifically for work in the ice; among other things lacking, her rudder could not be unshipped nor her propeller taken off when beset in the ice.

Garlington's instructions from the Chief Signal Officer called attention to the absolute necessity of reaching Greely that year. "This necessity cannot be overestimated as Lieut. Greely's supplies will be exhausted during the coming fall. Unless the relief ship can reach him, he will be forced with his party to retreat southward by land before the winter sets in." It was emphasized that Garlington was to communicate with Greely at all costs. In case the vessel could not get up to Lady Franklin Bay, Garlington was ordered to land his party and stores at or near Life Boat Cove, discharge the relief vessel and remain with his party until the following year. In case his vessel should be unavoidably frozen up in the ice pack, he should proceed to Cape Sabine in personal charge of the party and push north until Greely's party was met. In carrying out his duties he was to be bound by the instructions of Lieut. Greely dated August 17, 1881, a copy of which he was given. This specified where the caches should be left.

Garlington proceeded to St. John's on board the *Yantic* under Commander Wildes. During this trip, they discussed the relief expedition and made arrangements for their future action. On arrival at St. John's, they met Lieut. Colwell of the Navy, who had volunteered for duty with Lieut. Garlington and was assigned to his command.

They found that a great part of the supplies had already been loaded on the *Proteus* in a haphazard manner, with no markings on the cases to indicate which contained food, scientific instruments, arms or other equipment; so it was necessary to unpack and mark the boxes, repack and rearrange them before starting. This was the first delay.

The *Proteus* had been hired rather late in the year and its crew had been taken from men who had not already been engaged to go to the sealing grounds, so that the best men were not available

On June 29, the *Yantic* and *Proteus* left St. John's for the north. The *Proteus* reached Godhavn on July 6th, under steam, and waited for the *Yantic,* which did not come until July 12th, under sail. This was the second delay. The *Yantic's* bunker capacity for coal was so limited that sail had to be used as far as possible to conserve the fuel supply.

From this place on, the *Proteus* pushed ahead of the *Yantic,* and worked her way through ice to Littleton Island without much trouble, but did not stop there. Reaching Payer Harbor (at Cape Sabine) on July 21st, Garlington went ashore and found the cache left the previous year by Beebe, everything in good shape except that the boat showed claw marks of bears and the tarpaulin covering the stores not under the boat had been torn by wild beasts. While at work around the caches, it was discovered that the ice pack to the north had broken and Garlington, returning to the ship, asked Captain Pike to steam north at once. They rounded Cape Sabine, keeping on through the leads in the broken ice until they arrived about four miles from Cape Albert. This was within 140 miles of Greely's party, and about two weeks before they started south. Captain Pike thought the ship could be forced through the ice to clear water beyond and began ramming the pack. It was ineffectual as the fragments of ice around the ship became so finely ground up that when the ship backed, this fine ice filled up the passage in front of her, acting as a cushion which reduced the effect of the blow when the ship rammed again; so about midnight this effort was given up.

Another lead was found to the eastward, in which the ship

made some progress until about 2 A.M., July 23rd, when they were beset and jammed in the ice, unable to move in any direction, and only 200 yards from open water. Captain Pike did not think the ship was in any particular danger. At 5 A.M. the ice separated and allowed them to enter the open water. Again they got within four miles of Cape Albert, when they found that the open lane they had seen the night before had disappeared and the solid pack ice was in its place. At this, they turned the ship about and attempted to escape the pack, steaming southward until 11 A.M., when the ice closed in all around them and held them fast until one o'clock in the afternoon; but as the ice was very much broken up, they were not afraid of a nip.

At 2:45 P.M., the ship was brought to a standstill again, within 400 yards of open water. The ice, from 5 to 7 feet thick, along the crack they were following, began to show signs of great pressure. The ship was in a dangerous situation and it was seen they would be nipped. Orders were instantly issued to have stores ready to throw overboard. The great pressure from the floe pushed the ice high up against her sides amidships and astern. Still the ship held; but at 4:30 P.M. the starboard rail gave way with a crash, followed almost immediately by another crash, when the ice forced its way into the starboard coal bunker. The deck planks began to rise and seams open up. The greatest efforts were now made to get the provisions thrown out on the ice and clear the boats from the ship. Many of the boxes thrown overboard went down into the water under the vessel, as there was a space between her starboard side and the ice. Men were put on the ice to try to catch these articles but about 30% of all the supplies sank in the water.

They had much trouble getting the boats clear, not succeeding until the ship began to settle and the alarm was given "She is sinking." At 6:50 P.M. every one left the ship. They were afraid that in sinking she might turn over on her side, thereby endangering their supplies already on the ice, so they were dragged away a sufficient distance to avoid it. At 7:15 the *Proteus* began to sink and slowly went down on an even keel. The sled dogs, which had been released, ran in all directions but seven of them were captured by one of the Eskimos. The ice broke, separating the supplies, men and boats, but by great efforts they were again gotten together.

The enlisted men under Lieut. Garlington, Lieut. Colwell and the surgeon worked hard, remaining calm and collected under great stress; but the crew of the *Proteus*, except the ship's officers, did practically nothing. They did not help save provisions until after their own personal belongings had been packed and safely put on the ice. Lieut. Garlington records that as soon as the stores began to go over the ship's side, the crew took possession of anything they fancied. Boxes were broken into and bags of clothing rifled and looted. The ship's officers made no particular attempt to stop this lawlessness. Garlington spoke to Captain Pike about it and he replied that "they were the worst lot of scoundrels he ever saw." The men in the crew claimed that they were shipped under the British law for a British ship and that their pay stopped when the ship went down. Their shipping articles therefore were no longer in force and they owed no further allegiance to the officers. Garlington knew that to control the crew he would have to use force and he did not have enough at hand to make a success of it. He therefore kept his own men and stores separate from the others and avoided any unnecessary controversies.

Captain Pike took three boats for his crew, and Garlington's party went in two whaleboats. They agreed to act together as far as possible and made for land. Lieut. Colwell succeeded in getting through with a boat and caching provisions about 3 miles west of Cape Sabine. This cache consisted of hard bread, tea, bacon and canned goods, estimated at about 500 rations, and some sleeping bags. Other unsuccessful attempts were made to get to the land, but Garlington's men were played out and the crew of the *Proteus* would do very little; so they took a rest about 5 A.M. on the 24th. Later in the day they attempted to make land, but few of the men knew how to row. Handling the boats on and off the ice was a difficult undertaking. One boat came near swamping when the plug in the bottom worked out, because the boxes of food rubbed against it.

The floe commenced moving rapidly eastward, away from the land, and they had to make haste to get everything off it. After many failures, the loss of additional supplies and the loss of all the dogs on the ice, the whole party landed at Cape Sabine at noon on the 24th. Boats were hauled up and made fast and a check-up of rations showed that they had about forty days' supply on hand. They cached a considerable quantity of clothing, some chronometers and other instruments at Cape Sabine, then made ready to leave.

It was now just thirteen days before Greely started his retreat to this same vicinity. Including the *Proteus* crew, there were thirty-seven men with Garlington. Besides their forty days' rations, they were within thirty miles of twenty days' additional food, and one hundred miles from six months' supplies; they had a chance to kill a good deal of game; and finally the *Yantic* and a Swedish steamer were known to be cruising somewhere near. Notwithstanding these things, Garlington took with him every ounce of food he could carry, loading his boats to the danger line.

Garlington decided to cross Smith Sound, leave a record at Littleton Island about the disaster to the *Proteus*, and try to meet the *Yantic* instead of waiting for her to come up. His reasons, he explained later, were that as Commander Wildes had orders not to enter the ice, he did not think the *Yantic* would cross Melville Sound; also, in the event of missing the *Yantic*, he hoped to meet the Swedish steamer *Sofia*.

On July 25th, early in the afternoon, Garlington set out across Smith Sound, soon encountering fog, snow and rain. Leaving Littleton Island, they rowed down the coast of

108

Greenland, having the experiences usual in these latitudes. While Garlington's party was working its way down the coast, Greely's party, only a few miles away comparatively speaking, was trying to get down through the dangerous waters of Kennedy Channel and Kane Basin.

The Garlington party passed enormous icebergs which frequently turned over or split apart with a sound like the explosion of a 20-inch gun. The weather was so foggy and cloudy that celestial observation was impossible until August 21st. Near Cape York, Lieut. Colwell's boat became separated from Garlington's and they did not meet again until the end of the voyage. On August 22nd, Garlington met some Eskimos who told him that Wildes, in the *Yantic*, had heard of the disaster to the *Proteus* and had cached some stores for them at Tessuissak. Piloted by an Eskimo, they went on down the coast to Tessuissak, picked up the stores (fifteen days' rations) and proceeded to Upernivik, the residence of the governor, who gave Garlington a letter from Wildes which stated that he considered it a serious risk to keep his ship in that high latitude at such a season and that he would remain in Godhavn until September 15th, no later, then would turn homeward.

In the meantime, Lieut. Colwell had made his way to Godhavn, a distance of 900 miles, traveling 39 days in an open boat. He reached there on August 31st, and found Commander Wildes, who immediately started for Upernivik, arriving there September 2nd. Garlington's party and the crew of the *Proteus* boarded the *Yantic* and proceeded to St. John's, N. F., where they arrived on September 13th. Even then it was not too late to equip another ship and go north again, but it was not done. The *Yantic* left St. John's on September 20th, arriving in New York September 29th.

Chapter X

THE HARD WINTER

IT was inexcusable to abandon Greely's party in the north, when it was known that they had not received any rations or outside help for two years; but it was even worse to tie them down to Cape Sabine and keep them hoping for assistance there, which was never sent. Had Greely known that he and his party could look for no further help, he would certainly, he says, have turned his back to Cape Sabine and starvation, to face a possible death on the perilous voyage along shore to the southward.

One can imagine the feelings of the men when they began to realize what was ahead of them. Still they faced the difficulties like true American soldiers and did the best they could. They kept hoping to find aid on Littleton Island, as they could not believe that the men on the *Yantic* had abandoned them without a supreme effort to reach them, either by boats or over the ice by dog-sleds and packs.

Rice and the Eskimo Christiansen went down to Cape Isabella to see if any cache had been made there, but nothing was found save the old Nares cache of 1875, 144 pounds of English beef, which they left.

On October 12th, Greely decided to move from Eskimo Point to Cape Sabine, instead of trying to drag the heavy

III

stores of food and equipment left there to their present camp, by man power. It was a hard trip of three days, the equipment having to be relayed and the trail gone over several times with a sled. Each day they worked about eight hours on the road and two hours loading, beginning before daylight and ending after dark. At night they camped on the bare rocks, with no shelter other than sleeping bags. As Brainard wrote in his diary, "One thickness of hide, frozen as hard as flint, cannot keep out the cold"—especially in a howling storm and below zero temperatures.

After looking over the ground near the cache made by the *Proteus,* it was decided that that place offered the best prospects for their winter quarters. Even with this cache, which contained only 100 rations of meat instead of the 500 mentioned in Lieut. Garlington's note, it was found they had not one-fourth enough food to get them through the winter. The only possible way of supplementing it was by hunting and gathering up what the country afforded, which was very little. The weather was getting colder and the men were exhausted by their strenuous efforts in this last move on reduced rations.

They commenced the construction of a house, 25′ x 18′ on the inside, with everybody working on it except one soldier and the two Eskimos, who were kept hunting all the time. The interior walls of the house were made of stones, and the outside covered with snow blocks. For a roof, a whaleboat left in a cache near by was laid across from end to end. Holes were cut in its sides and oars inserted, which reached to the side walls, and over this canvas was stretched, and then covered over with snow blocks. It was difficult to work very long at a time owing to the darkness falling so soon, it being past the middle of October. On the 19th, the party moved into the hut.

The roof was low, and the only place a man could stand erect or even hold himself up on his knees, was under the whaleboat. When they sat up in their sleeping bags, the heads of the tall men touched the roof. It was not built higher owing to the shortage of rocks, and insufficient hard snow for snow-blocks. When twenty-five men were in the room, in their sleeping bags, the only free space left was in the center where the cooking was done. Being so huddled together made them extremely uncomfortable. The thwarts in the boat were used as shelves for dishes and provisions. The door, three feet by four, which opened outward, was overhung by a piece of canvas to help keep out the weather. Just outside the door, a small storehouse for food was built of snow blocks.

After the hut was completed, Greely had the various caches in the vicinity collected and carefully checked over, to ascertain what each contained in the way of clothing, equipment and food. While the men were still hauling in supplies, in sub-zero temperatures, their weakened condition resulting from the meager diet began to manifest itself alarmingly. Brainard, who had been given charge of the food stores and the issuing of rations, opened a case of dog-biscuits to ascertain their condition and found them bad. He makes this significant entry in his diary:

> When this bread, thoroughly rotten and covered with a green mold, was thrown on the ground, the half-famished men sprang to it as wild animals would. What, I wonder, will be our condition when we undergo a still greater reduction in our provisions?

Three or four hunters were kept constantly in the field, but with little success on account of the darkness and violent storms. The rations, reduced to about one-fourth the amount men would normally eat, were pronounced by the doctor insufficient to support life, but it was decided this way was their only chance for survival.

By the end of October, the Greely party was realizing more acutely the fate that awaited it. They had no fuel except a scanty supply of alcohol, which was doled out for cooking; so they were always miserably cold and damp, and constantly hungry. The temperature of the hut never rose above freezing. About half the men were not fit for duty.

On October 24th, the sun disappeared at this camp, nine days later than at Fort Conger, so great a difference does a few hundred miles make in the length of the winter night.

No newspapers had been left by the Garlington Relief Expedition but some lemons had been wrapped in scraps of newspaper, which were carefully undone and smoothed out. Sgt. Rice read these aloud in the evening by the light of the "Eskimo lamp," and it was learned that President Garfield had died. This one lamp, a tomato can filled with seal blubber, with wicks made from pieces of rope and old socks, was all they permitted themselves, as they had hardly sufficient oil for it to last through the winter. Its light was fitful and wavering at best, but they could only afford this poor illumination for a few hours a day; the rest of the time the men had to grope around in darkness.

Their cookstove was a small sheet iron cylinder, made by one of the men from the iron with which the whaleboat was sheathed. Soon the alcohol for cooking was almost exhausted, and they had to eke it out with pieces of barrels in which the food had been cached, and a broken old whaleboat they had found. In order to utilize this wood to the greatest advantage, it was cut up in pieces no longer than a match.

Judging from their diaries, the thoughts of the men were not centered so much on themselves as on their families and friends at home. Was any one thinking of them and wondering about their fate? What was going on at home?

During October, feeling in the United States ran very high over the failure to rescue Greely, and his abandonment to death by starvation and freezing. Mrs. Greely, in San Diego, had hoped against hope that a rescue would be effected that summer, but now she knew that their chances for life were slight indeed. However, she knew Greely's indomitable spirit, his great physical strength and endurance, and his ability to handle men. With him she had studied all the data and information about conditions in the Arctic and was as familiar with the subject as any one could be who had not passed a winter in the north. She was undecided whether it would be best to go to Washington and attempt through personal solicitation to get something done, or to remain in San Diego and rouse the press of the country as much as possible, and endeavor through the Senators and Representatives from Massachusetts, Greely's home state, to get some action. She chose the latter course, as she knew that Washington was full of people continually importuning the President and Congress for a thousand and one things. She felt she would be lost in the shuffle in Washington, but outside it she would be much stronger. Her judgment was sound. The pressure of public opinion grew stronger and stronger to find out the facts and rescue the Greely party.

On October 31st, the President convened a Court of Inquiry to investigate the whole matter of the conduct of the Greely Relief expeditions and ascertain why the rescue had not been effected. The court met on November 8th, and after lengthy hearings, came to no conclusion at all, the usual action of a board. A few reprimands were given but nothing was done to get to the Greely expedition, which then of course was in desperate straits.

The question of another expedition was agitated in the press. Secretary of War Lincoln was credited with saying that he did not see any use throwing away more money for dead men, that they must have perished by that time. He seemed entirely unfavorable to another attempt at a rescue, as the first two had ended in such dismal failures. Mrs. Greely, however, felt they were still alive and she enlisted the active aid of Mr. Douglas Gunn, editor of one of the San

Diego papers. Mrs. Greely knew that Secretary Chandler of the Navy favored another relief expedition, so a newspaper campaign was begun for the organization of a Naval expedition to go up and get Greely. Mrs. Greely was convinced that an expedition by ship should be put in the hands of the Navy, not of private soldiers or lieutenants of Cavalry as had been the case before.

Douglas Gunn besought every paper in the country to help him. The terrible situation in which the Greely party had been left was vividly described. Every one who read the accounts was importuned to write to their Congressmen and demand that they take action and vote money for another expedition.

*   *   *   *   *

At Cape Sabine, the hungry days passed slowly by. By November 1st, all the caches had been gathered in with the exception of the 144 pounds of English meat at Cape Isabella. Up to this time Greely had refused to send any one out for it, knowing that in their weakened state those who conserved their strength would have the best chance for survival. This 35-mile trip, through darkness and fierce storms, over the broken, rough ice, besides the additional burden of pulling a heavy sledge, was a perilous undertaking for well-fed, hardy men in perfect health. What chance would his poor fellows have, half-starved, insufficiently clad and without proper equipment? But Rice kept begging to go, others volunteered and on the 2nd, Greely gave in and sent a party of four,—Rice, Fredericks, Elison and Lynn. They carried a light sledge, a four-man sleeping bag, a tent fly, rifle, cooking lamp and pot; and every other member of the party contributed some article of clothing from his poor scanty stock to keep them warmer. Their ration was a pound of food per day, eight ounces of meat and eight ounces of bread.

They started out in the Arctic night, at 8 A.M., in a temperature of 9 below zero. The first night out they had to camp on the ice, but the second they reached Eskimo Point and stayed at the old cabin. They reached Cape Isabella on November 7th. The sky was clear and the moon bright, and to the southward the water was open as far as the eye could see. Even at that season of the year a vessel could have reached them without disaster.

On the fourth day, they secured the meat and started back. Elison, contrary to instructions, insisted on eating snow, as his thirst was so great he could not stand it, and in this way he wet his mittens through. Eating snow in the Arctic is a very dangerous practice. It may allay thirst temporarily, but at the same time it increases a man's feverishness and lowers the temperature of his body. That day, on account of the difficulty of making their way over the ice foot of Baird Inlet, they were fourteen hours reaching their camp. They had expected to do this in a few hours, and started out with only a cup of tea and no food, consequently they were exhausted on their return. Here they found that Elison had frozen both his hands and feet.

Their sleeping bag was frozen hard as a board, but they lay down in it, and Rice and Frederick worked with Elison all night long, trying to thaw him out. He was in terrible pain and no one had any sleep; but in the morning, warm food and drink put new life in them all and they thought they could make it. They started out, but Elison had been frosted too severely, and he soon succumbed to the cold again. In a little while his legs became as hard and stiff as wood, so he had to be almost carried along by Frederick, while Lynn and Rice pulled the heavy sledge. The temperature fell to 25 below zero.

On the morning of the 9th, Elison became totally helpless. The others tried making double trips, first for Elison, then for the meat; but after wearing themselves almost to the point of exhaustion, they saw that it was a question of abandoning either the meat or Elison. Accordingly, they left the meat, which meant so much to them, there in the snow, sticking a rifle up beside it to mark the place.

After eight or nine hours' further struggle, they reached the Eskimo Point hut, where they made a fire out of the iceboat cached there, cooked a meal, dried their clothing and thawed out Elison. His suffering, which had been bad enough before, increased now so that it was the veriest torture.

As soon as possible next day they started out again, one man supporting and dragging Elison, while the other two pulled the sledge; but Elison's feet and hands froze again and his face also, so that even his eyelids stuck together.

Finally, when they reached a hill, his feet had become so solidly frozen that he could not stand. They were unable to haul Elison up the hill, so they had to camp in a northerly gale, which prevented their making a fire. It was decided to send Rice to the main camp, fifteen miles away, to get help. He started at once, eating some frozen beef on the way. The three men remaining lay down in the four-place sleeping bag and waited.

At midnight, Rice staggered into the cabin and could barely open his frozen lips to report to Greely, "Elison is dying at Rosse Bay." This was the first serious mishap to any of the party. Brainard and the Eskimo Christiansen were sent out at 4:30 A.M., temperature 28 below, with brandy and food, and were followed two hours later by Lieut. Lockwood and Dr. Pavy, with a large sled and four of the strongest men in the party.

The two men left with Elison tried to keep him warm with their own bodies in the sleeping bag, but as it was laid on the ice in the full force of the gale, it froze quite stiff after a few hours, so that the men could not get out or even turn over. They had to lie in the same position for eighteen hours. During all this time, they had nothing to eat or drink, and poor delirious Elison groaned and screamed with pain hour after hour. They did not know if Rice could make camp or not, in one march; if not, he would certainly freeze, having no sleeping bag, and in that case they would die, too, lost in the Arctic wastes. With all these horrors, it is no wonder that Lynn's mind gave way. He talked incoherently and clawed at the fastenings of the bag, trying to get out to no avail. He never regained his reason.

Finally, the rescue party came up and one can imagine with what intense relief they heard Sgt. Brainard's voice over them. He had to cut the bag apart to get them out, and their clothing was frozen so stiff that they could not stand alone. After giving Elison some brandy, Brainard prepared a warm meal for them all, and after a while Frederick and Lynn were able to start off to Camp Clay without assistance. Lieut. Lockwood's party came up and Elison was placed on the sled and brought in. His hands and feet were frozen solid and his face was in such bad condition that he did not look human. For a week he begged to be put to death but after that he regained his composure and became as cheery as any other member of the party, although still in great pain.

This rescue was a wonderful feat. The eight men, feeble and exhausted as they were from want of food, had made a journey of forty miles in 44 hours, traveling over rough and heavy ice, at temperatures ranging from 19° to 34° below zero. For the last leg of the trip, Brainard was continuously on duty for more than twenty hours, marching and pulling the sledge, which was the hardest kind of labor. He remarks in his diary:

Of the condition of the sledgers, I can speak only for myself. I am probably one of the strongest, but at no time in my life have my physical powers been called on to sustain such a trial as last evening. Even my will wavered.

This was quite an admission for the brave and sturdy Brainard, the modest chronicler who habitually understates his miseries and wretched privations.

Chapter XI

DEATH VISITS CAPE SABINE

IT began to be suspected that one of the party was stealing food. Lieut. Lockwood discovered an open full can of milk hidden away. Later it was established that the marks on the tin corresponded to those made by a knife belonging to Private Henry.

The men were inclined to keep in their sleeping bags for longer and longer periods, and it was hard to get them out. In order to occupy their minds and keep them from dwelling on their desperate condition, Greely began to give daily lectures of from one to two hours on the physical geography and resources of the United States, followed by similar talks on each state and territory. Israel talked on astronomy, and Dr. Pavy about France, natural history and physiology. In the evenings, some one usually read aloud from one of the six or seven books in their "library": "Pickwick," "Coningsby," Hardy's "Two on a Tower," Hayes' "Polar Sea," "A History of Our Times," "The Life of St. Patrick," the Bible, and Army Regulations, a copy of which was left for them in the wreck cache!

November 29th, the last Thursday in the month, was indeed a sorrowful Thanksgiving, but they scraped together all the delicacies possible and celebrated the day. In the morning, a double ration of coffee was issued; for lunch, a fox stew with bacon was followed by rice pudding, chocolate and seven ounces of hard bread to each man. Twenty-five gills of rum and twelve lemons made a fine punch. For the first time since November 1st, Brainard records, they had a feeling of repletion after eating; and he adds with perfect sincerity that the day had been the most enjoyable of his life! Songs and merriment kept up until midnight. Greely mentions in his diary that the Psalms read that day made a deeper impression than he had ever noted before.

On the night of December 4th, Greely was awake and heard Dr. Pavy steal bread from Elison's bread can. As he was the only surgeon in the expedition and medical attendance was required in ever-increasing measure, Greely felt it necessary to effect no open breach and spoke to no one about it except the next two in command. It was only the iron discipline of the army, their self-control and their regard for one another that kept these starving men from eating up anything they were strong enough to take. The ration they were getting was just enough to keep the gnawing pangs of hunger always alive and at their strongest, with no surcease such as comes when a man has abstained totally from food for a time. They were hungriest just after eating, and it was worse when they were eating fifteen ounces a day than when they were eating ten.

The only game obtained during these dark days were foxes. Every few days they got one, weighing from 3 to 5 pounds. Every bit of the fox, even the intestines, was eaten, and no one ever expressed any repugnance. The heart and liver always went to the hunter as a reward.

As in previous years when the sun began to come north, although there was no perceptible change in the light at first, it had a strong influence for the better on the party. Each day now grew lighter. Christmas was celebrated with a seal stew, consisting of seal blubber, potatoes and bread, flavored wth pickled onions, followed by a rice pudding with raisins, seal blubber and condensed milk, and a punch made of half a gill of rum and a quarter of a lemon to each man. Everybody was required to sing a song or tell a story and they were regaled with Danish, French, German and English songs and the peculiar, sweet native melodies of the Eskimo.

The spirits of the men were keeping up in a remarkable manner. Dr. Pavy reported the entire party in an excellent state of health, considering the ration they were living on.

To augment their rapidly diminishing fuel, they began burning rope to cook their meals, which made a dense and pungent smoke irritating to eyes and throat. Cooking became a very trying job. The ceiling being so low, the room soon filled with steam and smoke. Most of the men put their heads inside their sleeping bags until the cooking was completed but the poor cooks had to stand it. It was necessary for some one to blow constantly on the fire to keep it alight.

During January, many began to show signs of decided weakness. First Elison's right foot, then his left, sloughed off and the doctor cut just a fragment of skin that was holding them. Elison never knew it had happened. The doctor also amputated some of his fingers. In spite of his terrible freezing, it looked as if he would live.

Brainard discovered a hole cut through the canvas roof of the storehouse, and found that some one had broken into a barrel of bread and taken out several pounds. Henry was again suspected of the theft. He was a very big man, his weight being 204 pounds at the time he joined the expedition, and he was consistently keeping his strength while the others grew weaker. If he kept stealing food, he would soon be able to do up any of the rest of the party or all of them combined. In contrast to his behavior, Brainard, weakening from overwork, was offered an extra allowance of an ounce of bread daily, but refused it, saying he would take his chances with the rest.

Toward the middle of January, they began burning boot soles for fuel. The scientific observations continued to be made, regularly and carefully. They started preparations for crossing the sea to the Greenland side as soon as it should become light enough to travel. Greely felt sure that the strength of the men would not allow any such undertaking unless some miracle happened, still he went ahead with the arrangements to distract the attention of the party from their terrible plight, and keep them thinking there was some means of escape from it.

On January 18th, Private Cross died. The doctor reported to Greely that it was due both to scurvy and starvation. So as not to depress the others, Greely told them that Cross's death was due to dropsical effusion of the heart, which was true, but this is caused by starvation. From that time on the doctor began examining the mouths of the men every day for symptoms of scurvy. Cross was buried with full military honors, except for the three volleys over the grave, on account of the necessity for conserving ammunition. It was the day before Cross's fortieth birthday and it was found that he had saved up a quantity of bread and butter for the purpose of celebrating it.

Greely found it necessary to forbid the practice of eating tea leaves left over after the tea had been made, as it was found to be injurious to health. It was again discovered that some one was stealing, when twelve cans of milk were missed on a periodical check-up. The feeling was so intense that Greely felt it necessary to counteract it by increasing slightly the allowance of seal blubber and hard bread, and he writes that "they hailed it with such joy and pleasure as would seem incredible to the rest of the world."

Greely decided to send Rice and Jens the Eskimo to Littleton Island, as a forlorn hope for bringing relief, still hoping that a steamer had gotten through and cached supplies there. He began feeding them extra rations so as to build up their strength for the journey. Elison, the frozen man, was also getting extra rations to keep him up. Some of the men, although growing very much weaker, began to save their food, but they were ordered to eat their full allowance every day. The temperature during January stood around 40 below.

Lieut. Lockwood showed decided signs of weakening, his

mind wandering quite frequently now, and he talked to himself a great deal about his favorite dishes. About this time, Brainard's diary reads: "Lockwood growing weaker and weaker. His fitful moods almost break my heart. As I watch him, tears gather in my eyes and there is a lump of sorrow which almost bursts my throat. That this should be the strong, daring and enthusiastic Lockwood with whom I went to the 'Farthest.' He said to me a few days ago, 'Brainard, I have lost my grip.' Pitiful, pitiful. It's true, too. He has lost the last hope of life."

By the first of February, four months' darkness had been passed and 24 out of 25 men were still alive, 22 of whom were in fair condition, confident and hopeful. It looked as though they might be able to last out until relief reached them.

On February 2nd, Rice and Jens started on their trip to Littleton Island. The day was bright as the sun would be shining in about two weeks. A blue fox was killed by Long, the hunter, just before they left, which was considered a good omen. Their outfit and rations were the best the party could give them. They carried packs on their backs, Rice forty pounds and Jens thirty-five. Many of the party thought they were going to certain death and for the next few days every one discussed their chances. It was hoped that if Rice failed to find a cache at Littleton Island, he would push on down to Etah and get help from the Eskimos there.

Brainard, who next to Greely was the hero of the expedition, fell ill, and the doctor diagnosed his swollen face and

PALAEOCRYSTIC BLOCK, LADY FRANKLIN BAY, JUNE 1882

"DISCOURAGING OUTLOOK"
A Picture Taken by Sergeant Rice

limbs as symptomatic of kidney trouble. Unless he avoided exposure to the cold and violent exercise, he was in danger. His loss would be a terrible blow to the party, as he was not only absolutely fair and careful in his work of measuring out the rations, but he was always ready to volunteer for extra duty; and he had the confidence of every man.

On February 6th, much to every one's surprise, Rice and Jens returned. They had struck open water, which stretched as far north as they could see, making it impossible for them to get over to Littleton Island. They reported much moving ice and dense water clouds along the edge of the fast ice, and said they were unable to see the Greenland coast. Both were exhausted, especially the Eskimo, but appeared well otherwise. For two days they had been almost without water, as their improvised cooking lamp would not work properly.

Their failure to get through was a bitter disappointment to the party, and Greely increased the rations slightly to counteract the ensuing depression, "a pitiful game of brag" as he calls it. Of course a little later he had to cut down to make up for this increase.

However, active work went forward on the proposed expedition to Greenland, to be undertaken about March 1st. All the gear was checked over and a list made of the weights that must be hauled or carried. An inventory of the rations showed that they could live until April 10th if they could make out on four ounces of meat and eight ounces of bread daily. On February 8th a cold snap froze the mercury and encouraged them to hope that the ice in Smith Sound would freeze over; but later they could plainly hear the roaring of the ice in the straits.

Scurvy again threatened some of the men, among them Lieut. Lockwood. Toward the middle of February, the tempers of the men became quite savage and frequent violent disputes had to be settled by Greely. "But," he records, "bitter talk sometimes relieves the mind, and no blow has ever been struck—a remarkable record for 25 tortured and irritable men, who have not known a moment of comfort in many months."

The men were becoming very dirty, their faces black and their clothes covered with grease and soot, but there was no way to get clean. For over a month they had had no water even for drinking, only for cooking and tea; they had to melt ice for this, as their water hole had long since frozen over thickly. Henry was again suspected of stealing food when some butter disappeared. Greely was becoming very anxious over Lieut. Lockwood's condition and at this time designated the succession of command in case both he and Lockwood passed away. On February 17th, the last of the seal meat, onion powder, peas, beans, carrots and corned beef were used up in a stew. On the 27th, the last of the onions, dog biscuit and coffee was reached. No trace of any kind of game could be found at this time.

On March 1st, the day set for crossing to the Greenland side, the straits were wide open, with no ice on which to walk. If the men had been strong enough to remove their remaining boat from its position as the roof of their hut, they might have attempted a combination boat and sled trip, but this was beyond their feeble powers.

On March 5th, the last of the seal-blubber, corn, tomatoes, potatoes and soup was issued. A gale of wind, with driving snow, sent the temperature in the hut down to 19° and it was with difficulty that the men could sleep more than an hour or two a day. From March 6th on, they were to have but 56 ounces of bread weekly, no dog biscuits or vegetables. Men in these circumstances talk constantly of food, the meals they have had at home and the menus they have read in restaurants. The only bacon left was rancid but they ate with relish both the bacon and the tallow in which it was packed. They even scraped the stearine away from the copper candle molds, covered with verdigris, and ate it.

Hunting parties were sent out as some signs of game were noticed. Bear and fox tracks were seen, and a couple of ptarmigans, but none was killed.

On March 8th, the first hair-cutting of the winter was done. The men crawled to the foot of their sleeping bags and a barber passed along the alleyway snipping off the matted masses of hair.

Toward the middle of March, the strength of the party diminished noticeably; two could not walk and half a dozen could not haul a pound. Long and Christiansen made a long trip to Alexandra Harbor to hunt, a former Arctic expedition having recorded that many signs of game were seen there; but they returned three days later, after covering 70 miles, exhausted and unsuccessful. On the trip, their sleeping bags froze up so tightly that they were unable to get into them farther than the hips. This was the beginning of the end for the Eskimo. He never recovered from the exposure and day by day his strength slipped away, despite an increase in rations. Greely especially was very disappointed over the result of the trip, having counted on game, and admitted in his diary that it drove him almost insane to face the future. "To die is easy, very easy," he wrote; "it is only hard to strive, to endure, to live."

Rice and Frederick offered to go in search of the cache of English beef which they had had to abandon in November, but Greely decided it was too small an amount to justify the dangerous journey. Brainard killed three ptarmigan on March 14th, which were eaten entirely, beaks, claws and entrails. Toward the end of the month it was found that shrimps could be caught and a few were obtained from day to day by Rice and Brainard. These tiny crustaceans, known as "sea fleas" or "sea lice" by the whalers, are only about half the size of a housefly, and are half shell. It took 700 of them, by actual count, to weigh an ounce; 1300 would about fill a half-pint measure. The "baits" which the men employed consisted of sealskins sewed over large stones, which were put into nets and thrown into the water. The shrimps collected on the surface of the skins and were then scraped off.

On March 24th, the whole party barely escaped being asphyxiated by fumes from the alcohol lamp on which breakfast was being cooked (the wood was all gone by now), the cook having forgotten to remove the rags stuffed into the stove pipe at night to prevent the entrance of cold air. Nausea and dizziness assailed the men and several fainted before the cause was discovered. Sgt. Gardiner, first to ascertain it, shouted, "It's the alcohol, open the door, open the door!"

All who were able tried to get outside, but some fainted before they reached the door; they were luckier than the ones who got out, as no sooner had they reached the open than they fell unconscious in the snow and as it was 25 below zero, they suffered severe frost bites before they came to.

It was noticed by all that every man tried to help his neighbor with the exception of Henry, who seemed quite unconcerned with the others' plight. Greely's hands were so badly frozen that for a week thereafter he could not even feed himself. Brainard fell down and got up, only to faint again, at least a dozen times, and next to Greely was the worst affected. In spite of his frozen fingers, after an issue of rum and bread all around, he went out with his gun and killed a five-pound fox.

When preparations for breakfast were resumed, it was found that some one had stolen a large piece of bacon from the pot, during the confusion. Suspicion pointed to Henry and everybody watched him. Shortly before lunch he complained of nausea, then threw up quantities of half-chewed bacon, whereupon his crime was revealed. In his haste to get the bacon eaten before being apprehended, he had almost swallowed it whole and this was more than his famished stomach could bear. Afterward, the Eskimo Jens, "our little man" as he was affectionately called, asserted that he had seen Henry steal the bacon, enacting in vivid pantomime the guilty man's manner of doing it.

A general investigation of Henry's conduct, held on the 25th, established the fact that he had not only stolen the bacon but rum also. The whole party was consulted and each man in turn pronounced him guilty. The men wanted to take extreme measures with him at once, but Greely decided that as it was a military command, he would deal with him as he saw fit. Having spared the medical officer on a previous occasion, he was unwilling to treat an enlisted man more severely, and announced that he would put Henry under arrest and require him to be always under the supervision of one of the men, except when he was in his sleeping bag. A few days later, ten ounces of English chocolate, which Brainard had found and was saving for Elison, disappeared, and circumstances again pointed to Henry as the thief.

On March 25th, for the first time since the hut had been constructed, a ray of outside light entered it, giving the party renewed confidence.

Brainard, Rice and Long were now the three most active men, shrimping and hunting whenever they could. Christiansen and Jens, the Eskimos, were not able to keep up to the same extent as the white men, in this race with death.

On March 27th, Greely's fortieth birthday, Long succeeded in killing 38 dovekies, 33 of which Jens retrieved with his kayak which he had carried along all through their wan-derings and privations. This was a wonderful boon to the starving men, and cheer after cheer were given the hunters as they came in with the game. On the 28th, Rice caught 27 pounds of shrimps; almost every day they took several pounds in the nets.

Poor Elison asked the doctor if he could not do some-thing for his feet, as they itched so uncomfortably. He did not know that both his feet had been gone since January.

Chapter XII

FORTY-EIGHT HOURS TO LIVE

DURING April, the strength of the men began to ebb alarmingly. Christiansen the Eskimo died on April 5th from plain starvation. On the 6th Lynn died, asking for water. It was noted in subsequent cases that the men kept asking for water from twelve to six hours before they died.

On this day, Rice and Frederick started out to attempt to recover the English beef abandoned on the Cape Isabella trip, to save the life of Elison. Greely had refused to let them try it before, but now the desperate straits of the party induced him to consent. The two men asked only that they be allowed to make the trip on the same ration issued to the rest of the party, 4 ounces of meat and 4 ounces of bread daily, but Greely made them take 6 ounces each. As Rice had been sick, Greely tried to dissuade him from going and let Brainard go in his place, but Rice insisted he was strong enough to make the trip and that besides he was more familiar with the country.

The sleds and sleeping bags for Rice and Frederick were hauled ahead by others of the party, and the only bag left was the one in which Lynn had just died; so Rice crawled in with his dead comrade and slept soundly until ready to leave. Of the farewells, Brainard writes:

The silent prayers of those who remained went with them, and eyes, to which tears were strangers, were dimmed with the love and fear we felt for these two brave souls. Weak and despondent, they go out alone in the bleak wastes of an Arctic desert taking their lives in their hands, to bring food to their starving companions. Before them lie famine, indescribable cold, torture to their minds, and then, perhaps, failure. And in the hut we must wait for the end of the story.

Soon after they started, they ran into high winds and blinding snow. Having no other shelter, they put their sleeping bag on the ice and crept in, eating a few ounces of frozen pemmican. They had to remain in the bag twenty-two hours, owing to a raging storm, during which time they were completely buried by snow. When they finally got out, they were so cold they had to travel for an hour to get warm enough to make a fire, but at last they succeeded in doing so, making some tea and cooking a warm meal. They had been thirty-six hours with nothing to drink.

Reaching the old camp at Eskimo Point, they decided to drop their sleeping bag and part of the rations there, as they knew the meat cache was only six miles further on. They hoped that with their lightened sled they could get to the meat and return in one march; but unfortunately, open pools of water caused long detours, they wet their feet and their footgear froze solid. A northeast gale sprang up.

At last they reached the place where the meat had been left, but in spite of a very careful search, they could find no trace of it, or the rifle that marked its position. No sign of their old sled tracks could be seen. From this, they concluded that the ice must have moved and carried away the meat.

Frederick wanted to go back at once to their sleeping bag but Rice was in favor of staying in the hope that the weather might clear up and enable them to locate their meat. For about an hour more they searched when suddenly Rice commenced showing signs of alarming weakness. They halted and Frederick gave him some spirits of ammonia in rum and made some tea. Even after warm food and drink, Rice was too weak to stand and his mind began to wander, reverting to home and friends, and all the food he intended to have when he returned. In lucid moments, he realized the condition he was in and told Frederick what to do with his personal effects.

Frederick took off his parka and wrapped it around his friend's feet. Holding Rice in his arms, he tried to revive him, but he died about 8 o'clock that evening. Up to the last few minutes, they laughed and joked together, as they had always done. It was almost second nature with them now, having looked death in the face so long, to continue to outface him boldly, with grim gayety and fun-making. Greely's journal continues the story:

"Frederick's condition may be more readily imagined than described. Starved by slow degrees for months, weakened by his severe and exhausting labors, chilled nearly to numbness, he was alone on an extended ice field with his dead comrade. His sleeping bag was miles from him and to reach it he must struggle against a cutting blast filled with drifting snow.

Such a march might well daunt the strong and hearty, but to that weak starving man, it must have seemed torture and destruction. For a moment, he said, he thought he must lie down and die; it was the easiest thing to do. But then came to him the recollection of his starving comrades, who awaited his return with eagerness and hope. If he came not, some of those behind, he well knew, would venture forth and risk their lives to learn tidings or bring succor. Thus thinking, he turned away from the dead to return to us...."

Across those lone snow-fields the little Frederick trudged doggedly, pulling the sledge for the seven miles that intervened, toward the Eskimo Point hut. There he found his sleeping bag frozen, and he was too weak to force it open till he had lain down awhile and taken some rum and ammonia. The next morning, revived by sleep and food, he went back to where he had left Rice's body, unwilling to leave it as the prey of hungry wolves. It was the work of hours to chop out a hole in the ice with his light ax; in it he laid the body of his friend and covered it over with ice and snow. Then by degrees, struggling and stumbling, he dragged himself back to the main camp. It took him four days, but he brought back everything they had hauled out; and what was most astonishing of all, he turned in Rice's proportion of the rations, which he had not touched. Rice's death made a profound impression on the rest of the party. They were fond of him and now felt that he had sacrificed his life for theirs.

Lieut. Lockwood, a brave, loyal officer, died on the 9th.

As there was no commissioned officer who could be designated second in command, Greely at this time revoked the order of August, 1881, relieving Lieut. Kislingbury from duty, and restored him to his former status. He complimented him highly for his work on the retreat from Conger, and subsequently, when he overworked and strained himself severely helping collect the caches. However, on the 14th, Lieut. Kislingbury was so ill and feeble, both physically and mentally, that Greely judged him unable to assume the responsibility and appointed Brainard his successor instead.

Jewell died on the 12th in Greely's arms. Greely had fed him for several days and tried to inspire him with new courage and hope, but he was too far gone.

On Easter Sunday morning, a snow bird lighted on top of the hut and chirped distinctly. Every noise was stilled as if by magic until the bird left. His coming was taken as a good omen, and cheered them up.

Brainard had been catching shrimps, bringing in twenty or thirty pounds a day, which with a little meat was made into a stew and kept the men alive. On April 11th he suddenly burst into the passage, shouting, "A bear! A bear!" and fell down in a faint. Lieut. Kislingbury, Long and Jens immediately started in pursuit, but Kislingbury was soon exhausted. Long and Jens caught sight of him, separated and got the bear between them. Jens wounded the bear in the paw, but as he was making for the open water, Long, appreciating the critical situation, threw off his cap and glove, took careful aim and put a bullet through the bear's head. A party went out with a sledge and brought the carcass in, which weighed 400 pounds dressed. This undoubtedly saved many of the party from death in the next few days.

"This fellow is our salvation," exulted Brainard in his diary. "Everything will be utilized—intestines, lungs, heart, head, etc. The blood which had flowed from the bullet holes over the ice was chopped out with a hatchet and saved. The liver, windpipe, feet and stomach (nearly empty) have been set aside for shrimp bait. . . . No words can express the rejoicing in our little party today."

Jens was given an allowance of rum and tobacco and Long was conditionally promoted to be a sergeant. The next day, Long shot a small seal which Jens got with his kayak.

On April 18th, a detailed report of the health of the party was made by the doctor. It showed that Kislingbury was in a critical condition and six men were in very bad shape. About this time, Greely's heart began to trouble him and he gave detailed instructions to Brainard who was to take command in case he died. Severe illness, marked general debility and deep depression of spirits were now the lot of all. Henry eluded the watch set on him and stole some alcohol on which he got very drunk. Eight extra ounces of meat were given Brainard to keep up his strength for hunting and shrimping.

On April 29th, Long and Jens went out to hunt, both in fine spirits. Early in the afternoon, Long came back alone, and reported that Jens, while pursuing a seal in his kayak, had sunk and been drowned, taking with him the only reliable rifle in the party, an Army Springfield. Long did his best to rescue Jens but he was dead in a few minutes. Jens was very affectionately regarded by the men, as he was always faithful and trustworthy.

On May 3rd, their last bread was gone. The men were becoming so starved and weakened and their minds so affected that discipline faltered a little, but Greely's great power over men was successful in holding them together. About May 15th the last of their regular rations was used up and they began a desperate effort to keep alive on shrimps, kelp, a few snow birds and what animals they could get. They tried eating saxifrage, a little Arctic plant that contained some nourishment. On May 19th, the last alcohol was issued and on the same day Ellis died, the first death from starvation in six weeks. On the 23rd, Ralston died.

A wall tent was pitched about 300 yards southeast of the hut, as conditions there had grown so bad that the doctor reported all would die in a few days if they had to remain in it, due to the melting snow which dripped continually on them. The weakest men were moved into the tent, being barely able to get to it. The temperature was beginning to rise, being around 40°, and the tent was found much more comfortable. Whisler died on May 24th. The last issue of rum was made on that day. Seven of the survivors were now helpless and Brainard seemed rapidly breaking himself down getting shrimps.

The men began to eat the sealskin thongs that served for lashings on the sleds. They seemed to be kept alive on nothing but their determination to survive. On the 27th, Sgt. Israel died. He had been fed personally by Greely during his last days. Dr. Pavy was detected taking iron from the medicine chest, and had been accused by several men of taking large quantities of Dover's powders, which contained opium.

On June 1st, Lieut. Kislingbury died. He became fully reconciled with Greely before his death. The last thing he did was to sing the Doxology and ask for water. On June 3rd, Corporal Salor died. Dr. Pavy acted more and more strangely, and showed signs of a final breakdown.

Many hours now passed between the scanty meals. Frequent fierce storms prevented the hunters from venturing out, and Brainard, while he kept at his shrimping whenever the weather permitted, was obtaining very few of them now, five or ten pounds every day or so. As he went to his shrimping grounds, he had to pass over Cemetery Ridge, by the graveyard. At first, he said, the sight of it made his reflections sad and gloomy. There lay his comrades and there he himself would soon lie beside them. The light was always caught by the bright brass buttons on Lieut. Lockwood's coat, which stuck up through the thin covering of earth they had been barely able to place over the dead. These buttons made him think of the better days at Fort Conger, when he and Lockwood were often together, and of the sorrow he felt at his death. But finally he became so sunk in apathy at the miseries of his daily life that he could pass the buttons without emotion.

Greely asked the doctor about eating lichens, which contain some nourishment, and Pavy recommended against it. Greely decided to try them anyway, so some were picked and eaten, first raw, then in a stew, which improved the taste. They also found and ate some reindeer moss.

Each man knew that death was very near. As a man was about to die, he passed into a stage of mental wandering without suspecting that death was about to overtake him. His companions knew it, however, and would look at one another, knowing that one more of their group was about to go. When they lay down to sleep, they were never certain that they would wake again. The only consolation was that each one died easily, without pain or suffering.

Their one blessing now was water. With the warmer weather, thawing began and they had fresh water in abundance, no longer having to melt ice for it.

Henry was caught stealing again and Greely decided it was necessary to take severe action, as the man was keeping up his strength to such an extent on the others' food that he could easily dominate the situation in a short time. Greely had a talk with him, warning him, whereat Henry promised to mend his ways and steal no more. Greely did not believe him and issued an order on June 5th to Sergeants Brainard, Frederick and Long, to the effect that Private Henry had been repeatedly guilty of stealing and that if he were detected again either eating food not issued to him regularly or storing or appropriating any provisions, he would be shot at once. The next day Henry was caught stealing shrimps

out of the messpot, and in addition to that, contrary to posi-
tive orders, he stole some sealskin thongs and sealskin from
the stores. He boldly admitted his thefts, no doubt thinking
he was so strong that nobody could harm him. Greely therefore issued an order in writing that he should be shot without further delay. The order prescribed that the three sergeants should decide the manner of his death by two ball
and one blank cartridge. Greely's idea was that these cartridges would be drawn by lot, that three rifles should be
loaded and the sergeants would not know which had the ball
cartridges and which had the blank. Greely, however, had
forgotten that the party had only one rifle left with which to
carry out the order; so the three sergeants drew lots to see
who would do the shooting, and bound themselves together
by an oath never to reveal the identity of the man who
did it.

When the time came for Henry's execution, he was near
the tent, on what they called Cemetery Ridge. Two of the
sergeants went to the vicinity of the old hut while the third
went up to bring Henry down, asking him to come and help
bring some supplies up. Suspecting nothing, he went along.
No one besides the three sergeants and Greely knew that he
was to be shot. Notwithstanding the advantage they had,
Henry was a very dangerous man. As he was so strong from
having stolen extra food, he could easily have disposed of
any number of the men in succession. Greely knew he would
take advantage of it at the slightest provocation.

The sergeants had considered making him stoop over by

a ruse, and shooting him in the back, but one of them thought it would be too ignominious a deed to shoot a man in cold blood from behind, and urged that he be given an instant to compose his soul before being dispatched. They therefore decided to tell him face to face that he was to be put to death in accordance with the order of the Commanding Officer. He was told to kneel and make his peace with God. This leniency was a mistake that almost proved to be disastrous. In front of him Henry saw the sergeant with a rifle, ready to shoot him. Looking around, his glance fell on an ax and he jumped for it, but one of the sergeants nearest put his foot on it. The two men were so close together then that there was danger of shooting the sergeant who had his foot on the ax, but the aim was true, and the bullet penetrated Henry's breast. He whirled around, yelling, "You have tricked me, you have tricked me!" Again a shot rang out, the second bullet went through Henry's head and he fell dead. This was about two o'clock in the afternoon.

Henry's previous record, unknown to the Greely party then, was a bad one. He had been taken with the expedition at the last moment, when one of the original members deserted just before they left the United States. In selecting another man, Greely went over the list of those who had volunteered and saw the name of Private Charles B. Henry, then on duty with the Fifth Cavalry, Fort Sydney, Nebraska. It was Greely's old regiment, and as Henry was the only man in the organization who had applied, and had been recommended by his Post Commander, Greely decided to take him.

Just before the departure of the Greely expedition, a photograph of its members was published in *Harper's Weekly*. One of the copies got to the officers of the 7th Cavalry, who recognized the man called Henry as a former soldier named Charles Henry Buck who had served in the 7th Cavalry in the early seventies. He had been at the Custer Massacre under Major Reno. Later he had been convicted of forging the signature of his troop commander to orders on the Post trader for whiskey and other things. For this he was sentenced to two years in the penitentiary. He escaped, and later killed a Chinese in a gambling fight in Deadwood, Dakota. After remaining out awhile, he enlisted in the Fifth Cavalry under the name of Charles Buck Henry, instead of Charles Henry Buck; so that if he had returned to the United States he would have had to serve out his sentence for forgery and probably would have been tried for murder.

After Henry was shot, the order for his execution was read to the remainder of the party, every one without exception agreeing to its necessity. As long as sufficient food remained, Greely would not adopt any violent measures, but when they were in such extremities as now, the stealing of even a little bit meant the death of one or more of the party.

Dr. Pavy was found helping himself to narcotics from the medicine chest, which it was believed hastened his end. He died on the evening of the 6th, the same day Henry was

147

shot, and at about the same time Private Bender died also. Both these men had stolen food. This left only nine in the party. They had not strength enough to bury the dead, but removed them a short distance from the tent.

Brainard and Long kept hunting and shrimping, and every one who was able gathered moss, lichens and saxifrage. It was decided to begin eating the sealskin clothing, but on getting it together, much was found to be missing. Schneider said that Henry and Bender had been eating it, and he had begged them to give him some but they would not. The rest of the party thought Schneider had been in the ring. Schneider's diary, however, had the following entry:

> Lots of sealskin and thongs were found on the Doctor and Bender both, which showed how dishonest they was. Although Henry has told before his death that I had eaten a lot of sealskin, yet, although I am a dying man, I deny the assertion; I only ate my own boots and a part of an old pair of pants. I feel myself going fast, but I wish that I would go yet faster.

On June 9th, about all most of the party could do was to crawl out on the rocks and scratch up a few lichens and what other vegetation they could find. Brainard caught a couple of pounds of shrimp, as without fresh bait they could take only a few. Elison, who had lost his feet and hands, was in the best health of any. On June 12th, Gardiner died. He had been thought to be one of the weakest members of the expedition, but his intense desire to return to his family had kept him alive thus far. In the morning, he was found partly out of his sleeping bag, holding an ambrotype of his wife and mother in his hands. His last words were "Mother! Wife!"

Brainard erected a distress flag on a prominent place to serve as a signal for any rescue party. At this time of year, the middle of June, the whalers usually reached that vicinity. A gale was blowing next day, and lichens and shrimps could not be collected, so the party began eating Greely's sealskin jumper which had been reserved for shrimp bait. Greely also cut off the dirty oil tanned cover of his sleeping bag and divided it between them. How men could exist under these circumstances is something to wonder about.

On June 16th, the shrimps failed them. It was impossible to get any now, unless some birds were shot for bait, as the old sealskin was practically useless. That day Brainard worked for five hours and took only two ounces. He did not carry these home. He was barely able to crawl back himself over Cemetery Ridge; and thereafter he went no more.

Schneider died on the 18th. On the 20th, Greely crawled out of the tent a few yards to get lichens, but a storm came up and drove him in. The next morning the gale was still blowing, and Frederick was scarcely able to cook the stew of lichens and heat some stewed sealskin, the remnant of Greely's filthy sleeping bag. The force of the wind was such that the tent gradually gave way, the efforts of the men in their weakened condition being unavailing to keep it up. By evening the front part of the tent was on the ground, pinning Greely, Brainard and Long under it, so that they could hardly stir. The storm continued unabated, with high wind and snow. Greely's diary ends here, the last entry being: "Buchanan Strait open this noon a long way up the coast."

On the 22nd, all were terribly exhausted and it was only due to the energy of Brainard or Frederick that a little water was obtained, which, with a little soaked sealskin, was all they had to eat or drink for forty-two hours. The end of all seemed very near.

Near midnight on the 22nd, Greely heard the sound of a steamer whistle blown three times. He could not distrust his ears and yet could not bring himself to believe that ships would venture along the coast in such a gale. Hope is a powerful stimulant, and when he asked Brainard and Long if they were strong enough to go out and look, they agreed to try. They could only crawl along the ground up the high, rocky slope where the signal flag had been planted. From the top they could see nothing, and soon Brainard rolled down the hill to report to Greely; but Long remained a few minutes, to attempt to set up their distress signal which had been blown down.

Back in the tent, Brainard discussed with Greely and the others where the steamer might be, and expressed as his opinion that the sound they had heard was the low moaning note the wind made when it blew over their water cans, just outside the tent. They were again resigning themselves to despair, when suddenly they heard running foot-steps, and a moment later strange voices calling, "Greely! Are you there?" They were rescued! And none too soon; if the relief party had delayed forty-eight hours more, probably not one would have been found alive. The seven survivors were Greely, Brainard, Frederick, Long, Elison, Connell and Biederbick.

Chapter XIII

THE RESCUE

WHILE the members of Greely's party were shivering, starving and dying at Cape Sabine, the outside world had not been oblivious to the terrible fate that was probably overtaking them. Mrs. Greely's efforts and the newspaper campaign had accomplished their purpose; and in the winter of 1883-4, Senator Dawes of Massachusetts introduced a bill which passed both houses of Congress, appropriating money for the relief expedition and also making provision for a prize of $25,000 to be awarded to any independent sealer or whaler who found the Greely party. Preparation of this expedition was turned over to the Navy and they went at it with a will.

The first step the Navy Department took was to convene a board of officers to recommend what should be done. This board was composed of General Hazen, Chief Signal Officer of the Army, under whom the other relief expeditions had been sent; Captain Greer of the Navy, who commanded the *Tigress* in 1873 in search of the *Polaris;* Lieut. Commander McCalla, one of the most efficient officers in the Navy, and Captain George W. Davis of the Army, as recorder. The board deliberated for a month and reported that the relief expedition should be controlled entirely by the Navy.

Three ships were selected, the *Thetis* and *Bear,* Dundee

steam whalers, and the *Alert,* one of Nares' ships in 1875, which was presented to the United States by the British government. On February 18, 1884, Commander Winfield S. Schley was selected to take complete charge of the expedition, his orders specifying that he should investigate the circumstances of Lieut. Greely's voyage to Lady Franklin Sound in 1881 and the attempts to relieve him in 1882 and 1883; that he familiarize himself thoroughly with the whole subject of Arctic exploration and relief expeditions; and that he should select his subordinates. These men, chosen from volunteers, were required to pass a rigorous physical examination. Schley selected Lieut. Emory to command the *Bear.* There was general approbation at the choice of Schley to head the expedition, and an equal amount in the case of Emory, who was known as a fearless and resourceful officer. Commander G. W. Coffin commanded the *Alert.* Each ship was also to have one officer with previous Arctic experience.

Letters poured in on them, among others one from old General Emory, who commanded a Corps in the Army of the Potomac during the Civil War, to his son:

My dear William—

The time is approaching when you will sail on your noble and chivalrous mission of trying to rescue from a horrible death a brother officer of a kindred service. I am now old and infirm and can do no good by coming to see you sail, and I might be an incumbrance.... That you may be rewarded for so noble and chivalrous a sacrifice to a sense of duty is the daily prayer of one who has but little right to pray, but who is sincere in making the prayer.

153

During the time the ships were fitting out at New York, Commander Schley and his wife were the guests of the Emorys at their country place at Roslyn, L. I. One night while Schley and Emory were discussing the expedition, Mrs. Emory in an adjoining room overheard Schley say to Emory, "Our orders are to bring them back dead or alive. Suppose we do not find them?" Emory replied, "In that case I shall not come back." This was characteristic of him.

The coal transport *Ybarra* was chartered and brought from Cardiff, Wales, with 2,000 tons of the best Welsh coal for these ships. A contract was entered into for a steamer, the *Loch Garry*, to bring 500 tons of coal from Cardiff to Littleton Island. The government had to assume all responsibility for the vessels from the time they left St. John's, Newfoundland, until their return to New York.

The *Bear* was put in commission on March 17th, the *Thetis* on April 2nd, and the *Alert* was already in commission when she arrived from England. As the *Bear* was more advanced in her preparation than the other vessels, Commander Schley on April 16th ordered Lieut. Emory to push north with all speed. He sailed on April 24th for St. John's, N. F., and as he left New York, the East River was lined with crowds wishing him godspeed. Steamers saluted, blew their whistles and the crews cheered. An intense feeling of interest and sympathy for the Greely party was manifested everywhere.

When the *Bear* left New York Harbor, she ran into heavy storms and dense fogs, but Emory pushed straight on, reach-

The "Thetus" Under Sail
Homeward Bound

Commander Winfield S. Schley

ing St. John's on May 1st, seven days out of New York. He remained there only long enough to make some repairs, take on coal and the dog teams procured for him by the American consul. Emory sailed from St. John's on a Sunday, coaling ship all that morning despite the indignant protests of the devout inhabitants who prophesied that God would not bless an expedition commanded by such an irreligious person. But after the *Bear* had gone, the Governor announced that Captain Emory had attended church service at dawn and told the priest that as his mission was to save lives, he considered he was not only justified but compelled to ignore the Sabbath; and the priest agreed with him.

Pushing through gales, much ice and fog, Emory reached Godhavn on May 13th, where he learned that several Scotch whalers from Dundee had started north ahead of him, spurred on by the American government's offer of $25,000 if they reached the Greely party first.

A little north of this Emory found the ice so heavy that he could not get through, so had to wait until a gale came from the proper direction to break it up. During this time he exercised his crew in abandoning ship on the ice-foot, in case the *Bear* was destroyed while in the ice-pack. Torpedoes were placed in the ice to test their effect in blowing it up. On May 21st, a northerly gale set in and the *Bear* pushed north again, right into the ice pack in Waigat Strait. They would go a short distance, then have to stop. Every advantage was taken of changes in the ice and weather to creep forward a little further.

On May 28th, he reached Upernivik and the next morning the *Thetis* arrived there. These two vessels then proceeded north together. Sixty days' rations were brought up and stowed opposite each boat on deck, to be used only in case of emergency. Knapsacks were issued to the crew, containing extra suits of underclothing and footgear, with orders not to touch any of them unless the ship was abandoned. Everything was arranged so they could act rapidly and precisely in case the ships were "nipped."

From Upernivik north, as every opportunity had to be taken to follow openings in the ice, the Commander usually took his place in the foretop, the officer of the deck in the crow's nest on the foremast, and a look-out on the end of the jib boom. The *Bear* led the way, ramming the heavy ice whenever necessary.

They reached Tessiusak June 1st, where they had to wait three days, then fought their way up to Melville Bay, where they were again checked and had to anchor to the ice. There they met three of the whalers, the *Arctic, Aurora* and *Narwhal,* that had worked their way ahead of the Naval expedition. On June 6th, they rammed their way through to some open water to the north and got ahead of the whalers. Night and day they watched for any lead to the north that they might follow, as they fully realized that every delay might mean a death in the Greely party, if indeed any were still alive. On June 11th, they found open water to the north and started off in a heavy snow storm, advancing only a mile or two a day. For the next few days, they were buffeted about by the ice, now here, now there. Some of the Scotch whalers caught up and got ahead of them for awhile.

They landed an officer and three men to communicate with the natives at Cape York and see if anything had been heard of the Greely party, but got no information. Entering Smith's Sound, they reached Saunders Island on June 20th. There they met a large number of natives, but these men knew nothing of the Greely party; they did not even know there were any white men in the north country. During all this time, men aboard ship constantly searched the shores with marine glasses for any indication of the party.

The *Thetis* reached Littleton Island on June 21st, but the *Bear* had fallen behind and Schley was much worried about it. The ships were now fighting their way through enormous bergs, running on uncharted rocks and getting stuck on the ice foot, but such was their strength that they were enabled by making slight repairs from time to time to keep right on.

Schley's men searched all the cairns on Littleton Island but found no word of Greely. To his great relief, the *Bear* arrived at noon on June 22nd. Lieut. Emory reported that he had been beset near Cape York for a day and a half, during which time the whalers *Arctic, Wolf* and *Aurora* showed up, but were unable to approach the *Bear's* position closer than three miles. The *Aurora* appeared to be nipped, since she lowered all her boats on the ice as if preparing to abandon ship; but on June 20th, a shift of wind slackened the ice and released the ships. Emory immediately pushed for the Carey Islands, in a blinding snowstorm, fighting for thirty-eight consecutive hours against the heaviest ice. On the evening of June 21st, the weather cleared and the Carey Islands could be seen about two miles off. No record of Greely was found there, so he sailed that night as he saw clear water to the north, and rejoined the *Thetis* on the 22nd.

The *Thetis* and *Bear* then sailed north for Cape Sabine, with a gale blowing. They reached Payer Harbor that night at 7 P.M., and moored with ice anchors to the harbor ice. Several parties were sent out to examine the cairns and caches, and at about 8 P.M. cheers were heard above the roaring winds. A few minutes later, Seaman Yewell came running to Schley, shouting that Greely and his party were at Cape Sabine. He handed the Commander several records which Lieut. Taunt had discovered in a cairn at Brevoort Island.

These records were found to refer to events eight or nine months before, and had been left there by Greely as he proceeded to his last camp on September 30, 1883. One had been left by Sgt. Rice on October 6th, and one by Greely on October 21st, which described exactly where the present camp was located.

A few moments after Yewell's arrival, Ensign Harlow signaled from Stalknecht Island, "Send five men, I have found all Greely's records, instruments, etc."

After Schley had read the records, he had a general recall of three long blasts sounded on the *Thetis'* whistle. (It was the sound of this whistle that Greely heard.) Lieut. Colwell was sent in the steam cutter of the *Bear* (called the Cub) to the Wreck Camp cache which he had established the year before, to tell the Greely party, if any were alive, that their relief was at hand. He was instructed to be very sparing with the food he gave them until the surgeons arrived. Schley then joined Emory on the *Bear* and steamed to the Wreck Camp cache about five miles from Brevoort Island. The *Thetis* was left back at Payer Harbor with orders to pick up all the parties sent out to examine cairns and caches, then to follow the *Bear* to the Wreck Camp.

The Cub reached the Wreck Camp ten minutes ahead of the *Bear*, which arrived at 9:30 P.M., followed by the *Thetis* twenty minutes later. As the Cub neared the Wreck Camp, its crew discovered a man standing on the rocks above the beach. It was Sgt. Long. They ran toward the shore and he stumbled and rolled down to meet them. He was a sad spectacle, with his long, matted hair, sunken cheeks, wild eyes and filthy clothing.

"How many are there left?" shouted Lieut. Colwell from the boat.

"Seven left," at last replied Long. He could scarcely talk and when he did, his voice was thick and mumbling and his jaws worked in convulsive twitches. He managed to tell them where the camp was, and repeated several times that the tent was down. While some of the rescue party started to Greely's camp, the others took Long aboard the *Bear*, where they gave him food and he told his tragic story: out of the original twenty-five, only Greely and six others were left alive, and they were now in camp, in "sore distress—sore distress"; it had been "a hard winter"; and "the wonder was how in God's name they had pulled through."

Schley writes: "No words can describe the pathos of this man's broken and enfeebled utterance, as he said over and over, 'a hard winter—a hard winter'; and the officers who were gathered about him in the room felt an emotion which most of them were at little pains to conceal."

Schley went on shore immediately in the steam cutter, taking with him Lieut. Emory, Ensign Reynolds, Dr. Ames and several of the crew of the *Bear*. The *Thetis* was signaled to send a party under Ensign Harlow with clothing, blankets and stretchers, and photographic equipment. Schley reached the Greely camp at 10 o'clock, finding that Colwell's party had partially raised the tent and had given the survivors a little bread and pemmican.

Schley went at once to Greely. The only way he could be recognized was by his glasses. Schley leaned over and patted his shoulder and said, "You are all right now, Major, we have come to rescue you." Schley then told Emory to talk to Greely.

Before the *Bear* had sailed from the United States, Mrs. Greely had written a letter to Emory at Roslyn, saying she was sure he would find her husband. She told him of Greely's devotion to Emory's oldest brother, Campbell, who had died. With this letter, she enclosed one for her husband and asked Emory to keep it with him always because she felt that if Greely were dying when found, her letter would bring him back to life. As Emory had no other copy of this letter, it caused him great anxiety. He finally had it sewn into the pocket of one of his pea jackets and told his orderly, "See that I have that jacket on when we find Greely."

Now he knelt down by Greely, and looking into his eyes, said very slowly, so he would understand, "Major, I am Emory."

Greely's eyes brightened up and he said, "Oh, yes, you are Cam." (Campbell had died before Greely went to the Arctic.)

Emory replied, "No, I am William. I have a letter from your wife—she and the children are well."

Greely's eyes filled with tears and he said, "Keep it." After awhile he said, "Put your hand in my sleeping bag and under me you will find my diary. Keep it." (This diary was burned up with many other valuable papers of Greely's in the San Francisco earthquake and fire in 1906.)

Emory was not able to deliver the letter until they were nearing Newfoundland, although he faithfully kept it on his person at all times. One day on one of his frequent visits to Greely on the *Thetis,* Emory, noticing he looked much improved, asked him if he didn't want Mrs. Greely's letter. "Yes," answered Greely, "I think I am strong enough now." The letter seemed to affect him profoundly.

Some time after midnight, the surgeons reported the party could be removed to the ships. A hurricane was blowing now and it was dangerous to work with boats, but it was considered more dangerous to remain where they were as the ships might be cut off by the ice at any time. Brainard, Biederbick and Frederick stood up and thought they were able to walk to the boats but they soon collapsed and had to be carried on stretchers, except Frederick, who got there assisted by two strong men.

In relating his impressions later, Commander Schley said that the scene, when they reached the tent, was almost impossible of adequate description. Greely was in his sleeping bag, with his body slightly inclined and his head resting on his hand. Although he had been told who the rescue party was, he appeared to think they were Englishmen. Physically he appeared the weakest of the party except Connell, but mentally he was more vigorous than any of them. His mind wandered to some extent. His answers to questions were disconnected and incoherent and his memory was rather indistinct. He would reflect for a moment and then say, "I am so glad to see you," then a moment later, "Those lemons your wife so kindly put up for us—." He had lain for weeks in his sleeping bag, on account of failing strength. Schley's description continues:

"He was unable to stand alone and was almost helpless, except in a sitting posture; all pain of hunger had ceased; his appearance was wild, his hair long and matted, his face and hands covered with sooty, thick dirt; his form wasted almost to a skeleton; his feet and hands were swollen, his eyes were sunken and his body barely covered with dirty and almost worn out garments which had not been changed for six or eight months."

Group around tent: (left to right) *Standing*, 3 members Schley's party. *Kneeling*, Lt. S. C. Lemly, Lt. E. H. Taunt. *On ground*, D. L. Brainard and H. Biederbick. *Bending over*, Surgeon E. H. Green. *Inside tent*, M. Connell. *In front of tent*, Com. W. S. Schley, Lt. W. H. Emory. *Group carrying* Maj. A. W. Greely on stretcher: (1) unknown, (2) Chief Engineer J. Lowe, (3) Chief Engineer G. W. Melville, (4) Surgeon H. E. Ames, (5) unknown, (6) J. Quevedo, Bosns Mate. *In foreground: By stretcher*, 2 unknown. *Facing front*, Ensign C. H. Harlow. *Man with furled flag*, unknown. *Right*, Ensign L. K. Reynolds and Lt. J. C. Colwell.

Connell's condition was critical. He was speechless and breathing with difficulty. He was cold to the waist, his eyes were fixed and glassy, and stimulants were administered to him with difficulty. His heart was beating irregularly, his temperature was low and his face swollen beyond recognition. He would have died in a few hours.

Elison was in his sleeping bag in which he had lain helpless for months, his hands and feet sloughing away. A spoon had been tied to the stump of his right hand so he could feed himself. He was in a better condition than the rest of the party as he had been allowed more food than they. If the rescue had been delayed forty hours more, he would probably have been the only survivor. His condition was a testimony of what these brave and generous men had done to feed an ill and injured comrade at the risk of their own lives.

Brainard, Frederick and Biederbick were so weak that they could barely stand alone. Their faces were also swollen and covered with sooty dirt, as they had not washed for eight months. Long was stronger because he had been issued extra rations to hunt. All the party knew what their swollen faces indicated, having observed this symptom in those about to die. When their joints and faces swelled up, it was a sure sign that death was not over forty-eight hours away.

No food was left except a mixture of lichens and strips of sealskin, and a few shrimps boiled into a repulsive, gelatinous mixture, which would not have lasted them more than forty-eight hours. All about the tent lay pieces of worn-out clothing, broken camp equipment and the bow of the boat that had been used for fuel. All the cherished possessions of the men had, however, been carefully wrapped up and marked, so they could be opened by friends or relations in case of death.

The vicinity of the camp presented a desolate appearance, bleak, barren and wild. On a little hill about one hundred feet away (Cemetery Ridge) was the row of graves, where the last ones buried had their heads and feet protruding, as their surviving comrades had been too weak to dig the graves deep enough.

Down in the hollow lay the deserted winter quarters, a wall broken down, with melting snow and ice pouring in. Back of the camp, and seeming to overhang it, were high hills of jagged, cruel rocks, covered with ice and snow, and beyond these, the eternal glaciers. On the ice immediately below the hut were found two dead bodies.

All speed had to be made to get away, but great care was taken in searching and finding everything of value. The bodies were exhumed under the direction of Lieut. Emory and wrapped in blankets, to which tags were attached showing the order in which they had been taken up. Emory drew a plot of the burying ground with the numbers of the graves marked, and the order of exhumation noted. This was submitted to Brainard who had had charge of the burial of the dead. The names of the dead were then marked on the tags and the identity of each was complete. All the bodies were recovered except those of Sgt. Rice and Jens the Eskimo who drowned, Sgt. Gardiner, Dr. Pavy, Corporal Salor and

Private Bender, the last four named having been buried in the ice foot and swept away by ice and tides. No trace of them could be found although careful search was made.

After gathering up everything they could find, the *Bear* and *Thetis* sailed about 3 A.M., going to Littleton Island, where arrangements were made to put the bodies in alcohol. Tanks were prepared and the bodies transferred to them on June 25th.

A few days after the rescue, Elison died. Proper diet had caused his digestion to function and restored the circulation of his blood, at the same time giving new life to the poisons in his system; gangrene set in, which necessitated a secondary amputation of his legs, and he was not able to survive this shock.

On the 26th, the *Thetis* and *Bear* fell in with seven of the Dundee whalers and notified them of the rescue, so they would be relieved of the dangers of further search. Schley bears testimony to the great knowledge that these men had of conditions in the ice, and their ability to handle their ships in it. The summer of 1884 was one of the closest and severest for many years. Great credit is due to Schley and his naval crews for having beaten these whalers to the Greely party. A few hours' delay would have meant the death of the survivors.

Arriving at St. John's, N. F., on July 17th, Schley immediately telegraphed the Secretary of the Navy, telling what had happened, and he and his men were highly complimented for their work. At St. John's, metallic caskets were made for the dead.

The *Thetis, Bear* and *Alert* sailed for Portsmouth, N. H., on July 26th, Schley notifying the Secretary of the Navy that he would reach there on August 2nd. Arrangements were made for his reception there. As the three ships left the harbor of St. John's, they were accompanied for a short way by a fleet of steamers with colors at half mast as an expression of sympathy for those who had died.

On Friday, August 2nd, 1884, four square rigged steamships rounded Fort Point at the entrance to Portsmouth Harbor, headed by the U.S.S. *Alliance,* the guide ship for three Arctic vessels of the Greely Relief Expedition. After it came the Arctic flagship *Thetis,* then the *Alert,* the supply ship presented by the British government, and last the *Bear,* all under Commander Schley. The whole Atlantic fleet had assembled to meet the Arctic squadron and render honors to the survivors of the Greely party and their rescuers.

The flagship of the North Atlantic squadron was the *Tennessee,* a large square rigged steam frigate. On board were Mrs. Greely and her relatives, Secretary of the Navy Chandler, Richelieu Robinson, General Hazen (Chief of the Signal Corps), Admiral Luce, Commanding the Atlantic fleet, and about one hundred army and navy officers, ladies and gentlemen. As the rescue ships proceeded up the harbor, the *Tennessee's* band played "Home Again." The sailors of the *Tennessee, Vandalia, Portsmouth, Swatom, Yantic, Alliance* and *Jamestown* manned the yards and cheered. It was a

166

wonderful and inspiring occasion. Flags and signals were displayed everywhere around the port, on merchant vessels and on land.

Soon after the Arctic ships dropped anchor, the Admiral's steam launch left the side of the *Tennessee* with Mrs. Greely and her immediate relatives on board. Mrs. Greely was a commanding figure, a tall brunette, young and extremely beautiful. At the companionway of the *Thetis,* she was met by Commander Schley who escorted her towards Greely's cabin. He asked her to wait until he informed Lieut. Greely of her arrival. At the sound of a whistle which Schley would blow, she could then enter the cabin. A minute later she heard the signal. Schley tried to escape the meeting but was not quick enough. He heard her cry "Dolph," then on his unwilling ears fell the sound of their mingled sobs.

For three years Mrs. Greely had lived in anxiety and uncertainty, beset by great disappointments and fears, but upheld by her constant belief that her husband would come back. It was largely due to her exertions that public opinion in America was roused to the point of demanding that the Greely expedition be rescued. It was a great day for the Greelys when they were reunited, an overwhelming vindication of the correctness of her intuition and a wonderful ending for her long desperately waged battle to force the relief expedition.

Shortly afterward, a lieutenant on the *Tennessee's* bridge sang out, "Commander Schley is coming aboard." A smoky looking little tub approached the side of the flagship, the very launch whose shrill whistle had sounded the message to the seven survivors at Cape Sabine that help was at hand. As it bore alongside of the handsome *Tennessee,* a smart little bit of a man energetically sprang up the companionway; it was Schley, who was greeted with cheers by officers and crew. Soon other launches arrived, bearing Melville, Seabury, Coffin, Emory, Norman and others. The congratulations lasted about two hours, then a review of the ships was held by Secretary of the Navy Chandler, General Hazen and Admiral Luce.

The *Thetis* was first visited. Lieut. Greely looked well, but like the rest of the survivors, seemed in an unnaturally fatty condition. Sgt. Frederick appeared to be the strongest. They were all under medical care with orders to avoid all confusion. Later in the afternoon they were taken to the Navy Yard and housed in comfortable quarters.

Next day Portsmouth was crowded with visitors from all over the country, who came by carriages, railway and boats, to honor Greely and the rescuers. Messages of rejoicing and congratulation poured in from the whole world, from the President of the United States and the Queen of England, who had loaned the *Alert.*

A parade was held, led by U. S. Naval Academy cadets from the training ships U.S.S. *Constitution* and *Dale.* The commanding officer of the cadets was Ensign Wm. F. Fullam. Following them were carriages containing the Greely party, the Secretary of the Navy, United States Senators, members of Congress, the Governor of New Hampshire and Army

168

and Navy officers. Then came various civic organizations, the Grand Army of the Republic, fire companies and several bands, one of which would play "Home Sweet Home," at which another would respond with "Auld Lang Syne." What created the greatest impression, however, were the men from the relief ships, who were turned out in Arctic clothing, sea boots and sheath knives, marching under the command of Ensign Harlow of the *Thetis*, Ackerman of the *Alert*, and Master Usher of the *Bear*.

Greely's wife and mother were in the reviewing stand, and as the survivors passed in front of it, they stood at attention.

Later all were served with a collation at the court house, and in the evening there was a large mass meeting at the local theater. Addresses were made by the Secretary of the Navy, prominent officials and Congressmen, General Hazen and Senator Hale. The latter said:

> Their story will be told to our children's children generations after we are gone. Their sufferings are no blot on their record and they will be placed forever among the immortals.

Otto H. Nesmith, Mrs. Greely's brother, read a response on behalf of Lieut. Greely and his companions who were too weak to attend the ceremony. It ended: "We thank you for your kind deeds, thoughtful consideration and tender sympathy to and for us all, the living and the dead."

Secretary of War Lincoln sent a telegram of congratulations but did not attend himself. General Benjamin F. Butler, ex-Governor of New Hampshire, made the concluding speech of the evening, to tremendous applause. He had dined quite well and made an extremely flowery address. "I am not connected with the Navy but come from the New Hampshire hills. . . . Heretofore the Red Cross of St. George has been planted for nearly 200 years nearer to the North Pole than any other nation, but now the free Americans have planted the Stars and Stripes further still, until that glorious banner, as it waves in the Arctic seas, will be mistaken by the wandering Eskimo, as they look to the north, for the Aurora Borealis." He then paid a glowing tribute to the Greely Arctic expedition and to the daring, courage, discipline and perseverance of the Navy in their rescue.

Lieut. Greely was tendered the use of a house which he occupied for the rest of the summer, while the other survivors were also comfortably housed while they recuperated.

The three ships proceeded to New York, the *Thetis* and *Bear* having covered some 7000 sea miles during this trip, and the *Alert* about 6000. The total cost of the expedition was about $750,000.

Greely's work was recognized throughout the civilized world and the scientific data obtained acknowledged to be the greatest contribution yet made to our knowledge about the Arctic lands.

Only a few years ago I ran into an interesting sidelight to this rescue, an example of how people all over the world were interested. While in Korea, I had dinner with Admiral Baron Saito, then governor-general of that province. In 1884, he was the Naval Attaché of the Japanese Embassy in the United States, and went to Portsmouth to welcome the

RESCUED AND RESCUERS

Greely party back. At dinner, the first person he asked me about was General Greely. He wanted to know how he was and what he was doing, and said he thought Greely was one of the greatest men living.

Greely did everything possible for his men upon their return. Biederbick and Frederick were discharged from the army on account of disabilities suffered in the Arctic. For Biederbick, Greely secured an appointment as Inspector of Customs in New York, and Frederick was appointed observer in the Weather Bureau at Indianapolis. Later, Long and Connell also received appointments in the Weather Bureau.

In 1886, Brainard was commissioned as a second lieutenant by President Cleveland, "as a recognition of the gallant and meritorious services rendered by him in the Arctic," the only instance in our military history up to that time of such promotion for excellent duty rendered in time of peace. Brainard, now a retired Brigadier-General, is still hale, hearty and active, a wonderful type of American soldier.

Chapter XIV

THE SIGNAL CORPS IN THE SPANISH-AMERICAN WAR

UPON Greely's return to duty with the Signal Corps in Washington, he devoted some time to assembling his scientific data and to rehabilitating his health. He was in a crucial mental state, very nervous, and the doctor told Mrs. Greely that he must be kept amused, that she would have to take him out a great deal. His hair was perfectly white, but later on it turned dark again. He had never. cared about social life, and it was very fortunate for him that Mrs. Greely was constituted as she was, an adept at human relations. He was a great celebrity, and they went everywhere, to dinners, receptions, teas, concerts.

Like any man in the limelight and prominent in public life, he received a great many letters from people he did not know, many of them cranks. He did not take them seriously, but when he found that Mrs. Greely did, he tried to keep them from her. However, she happened to get hold of one, from some man who thought he had a complaint against General Greely. In fact, he felt so injured that he threatened to kill the General. Mrs. Greely afterward told that she was terrified of this, and as she was under a perpetual strain in those days, her mind was not entirely sensible. Next to their house was a vacant lot, with a big "For Sale" sign on it. She became firmly convinced that the would-be murderer would station himself behind this big sign, and take a shot at the General some day while they were standing on the front porch letting themselves into the house. So whenever they came home and General Greely took out the key to unlock the door, she would edge over between the sign and him, so if the assassin was lurking there, he would have to shoot her instead!

Some months after his return, he asked for and received permission to go abroad, in order to accept the invitations of the French and German Geographical Societies and the Royal Geographic Society of Great Britain to lecture before them. This opened a very interesting period of General Greely's life, as it brought him into intimate contact with the distinguished men of Europe, the crowned heads of various countries, the great scientists, geographers and soldiers. Each of these Societies presented General Greely with their medals and testimonials, which unfortunately were later lost in his quarters at Fort Mason during the San Francisco earthquake and fire. These acquaintances and associations served him in good stead in later years, notably at the time of the Spanish War, when he wished to get information about the Spanish fleet. He knew exactly with whom to communicate in Europe and whom he could trust. He visited Gladstone and became quite well acquainted with him. He met Lord Rosebery, whom he liked and admired greatly; he had a letter from him just three days before he died, signed with a big "R" in a shaky hand, in which Lord Rosebery said he was not feeling well.

On his return from Europe, he continued on duty in Washington, and wrote his book "Three Years of Arctic Service," on which he made very little money. It was published by Scribners, in an expensive edition. Dorothy Drew, Gladstone's daughter, wrote to Greely that her father had requested her to tell him that his was the kind of book that should be in the hands of everybody, and it ought to be published in a cheaper edition; but Scribners did not see it that way. Mrs. Drew said further that Mr. Gladstone wanted Greely to know that he had sat up all night to read the book, and he had only done that with one other book in his whole life. Greely wrote back and asked what this other book was, and Mrs. Drew told him it was Wilkie Collins' "Woman in White."

In 1887, General Greely was made Chief Signal Officer of the United States Army, with the rank of Brigadier General. This was his first promotion since returning from the North. He had received no recognition or decorations from his own government. He was tendered, however, the "Thanks of the Commonwealth of Massachusetts," an honor that had only been conferred on one other person, of which he was very proud. He was not elevated to the position of Chief Signal Officer over the heads of any others, because he was the ranking officer of the Signal Corps. Grover Cleveland was then President of the United States, with Mr. Lamont as his Secretary of War, and in making the promotion, the President considered Greely's remarkable Arctic service.

Upon taking office as Chief, he completely reorganized the Weather Bureau, making it the leading meteorological organization of the world. Many of the instruments, pamphlets and studies used and followed now were instituted by Greely. He perfected certain self-registering instruments, and methods by which floods and storms were predicted and storm warnings issued. The Weather Crop Bulletin was initiated by Greely, which calculated for each locality and each month of the year the average rainfall and temperature, based on the readings of many years before, so farmers could gauge their planting accordingly.

In 1888, Greely published a book entitled "American Weather," which even today contains more accurate information on our weather than any other publication. Thirty years after its first appearance, it was still being used as a textbook by Professor Ward, in his course in Meteorology at Harvard University.

It was decided to transfer the Weather Bureau from the Signal Corps to civilian direction, under the Department of Agriculture. This was at the suggestion of General Greely who had always thought that the logical place for it; but upon its removal, it looked for awhile as if the Signal Corps would cease to exist. The older officers of the army, steeped in conservatism, thought that electrical means of communication were not as good as the mounted messenger, although every business man in the country was beginning to use the telephone. Bills were actually introduced in Congress for doing away with the Corps, but as these did not succeed, due to Greely's influence, the War Department made efforts to strangle it, just as both the Army and Navy are trying to do with aviation now. Every other nation in the world recognized the necessity for electrical communication and provided amply for it.

Greely continued working assiduously on developing suitable electrical and visual communication equipment for the Signal Corps. Among the great advances was an instrument called the "buzzer," which sent little jets of high voltage electrical currents into the wires, which were received at the other end in a telephone receiver. This instrument was able to work along wires as they lay on the ground without insulation, along barbed wire fences and even along railroad rails, under certain conditions. It was the precursor of the radio telegraph.

When everybody else had forgotten about balloons, Greely kept working at them, as well as kites and their accessories. He was the first to take up photography in the service and make a specialty of it. The field telegraph train was developed, which would keep telephone and telegraph wires with the troops as they advanced, far surpassing anything that had been done before. This turned out to be especially important during our Spanish and Philippine campaigns.

At the inception of the Spanish War, only $3000 was available to the Signal Corps for beginning the contest, and only eight officers and fifty sergeants composed it. General Greely plunged into the work of reorganizing the Corps, and his characteristic foresight and ability resulted in providing an able and efficient organization in the minimum time. The spirit that he engendered among his officers was wonderful. I, as the youngest officer in the Corps, remember distinctly his personal influence.

The Signal Company next to ours at Washington Barracks, D. C., was commanded by a captain, who, although an expert in telegraphic communications, did not know much about handling men. He had a junior officer under him who was very energetic but rather difficult to control. The captain wrote a letter to the Chief Signal Officer (Greely) requesting that the officer be relieved on account of his youth, inattention to duty and lack of experience. General Greely looked into the matter and sent back an indorsement to the following effect: "The application is disapproved. This officer's youth will disappear day by day; his inattention will be overcome by rigid discipline; and his lack of experience by careful teaching." The captain followed out these suggestions and the young officer turned out to be one of the best in the Corps. Greely's intuitive knowledge of men had shown him the worth of the young lieutenant.

At another time, a detachment of about 75 men from one of the New York regiments, en route to a southern camp, deserted their railroad train in Washington and seized the hotel American House, helping themselves to food and drink in the bar and kitchens. The men had been abandoned by their officers and had had nothing to eat for a couple of days.

They threw out a few policemen who came to arrest them, and the others knew if they tried to interfere, they would probably be seriously hurt.

A request was made to the War Department for assistance. A riot call was sent to Washington Barracks and I asked to be allowed to take the detail to arrest them. As I was the youngest officer, there was some hesitation about it, but finally they let me attempt it. I took fourteen enlisted men, commandeered a street car just outside of what is now the War College, and told the motorman to go up the track as fast as he could. When we reached the hotel, I dismounted the men, who were armed with 45 caliber carbines and ten rounds of ammunition, lined them up along the curb facing the building, and consulted with the captain of police who had the place surrounded.

Shouts and sounds of revelry came from within, but none of the men was visible. The police captain told me the soldiers were all drunk and very dangerous, and that anybody who went in would probably be killed. I reconnoitered the building and found there were only two means of egress through doors. I put an enormous private named Bell and another man before one door, and a man of equal proportions, Mickey Dugan, with a companion, in front of the other, with orders not to load their pieces, but in case any of the men attempted to escape, to knock them down with "butt to the front."

The proprietor of the hotel was in a terrible state, and said that his place was being torn to pieces, the guests were

178

all terrorized and it would hurt his business permanently. I took with me one man, a classmate in college, Robert Sterrett, (now Colonel Sterrett of the Cavalry) and placed Sgt. Travis with the remaining men as reserve, at the corner of Sixth and Pennsylvania Avenue, so he could act in any direction, with orders to reinforce either door and keep the men inside until I gave him directions to the contrary.

Sterrett and I then removed our weapons and walked into the hotel unarmed. The men were sitting about in the lobby, drinking out of bottles and taking it easy. I called "Attention," and seeing that I was an officer, they immediately stood up. I walked into the bar, a long room with a large mirror and many bottles just behind the bartenders. A remarkable scene presented itself. Several men who were ex-bartenders had gone behind the bar and were mixing drinks for the crowd. Once in a while somebody would throw a bottle through the mirror and everybody would laugh. The whole thing was so amusing, it made me laugh so that I could hardly call "Attention." When I did, all but two or three immediately stood. I asked who was in charge of the outfit and a small First Sergeant, about five feet five came up, and gave me a figure four salute, such as the British use. He had been a non-commissioned officer in the British service. I asked him where his men were and he said they were all there in the hotel except three. I directed him to fall them in, in four ranks in front of the bar and call the roll, which he proceeded to do from memory, as all old-time sergeants used to do. A few of them were in such condition that they could not stand up. Two or three tried to escape through the doors but were promptly stopped. No one had been hurt. The First Sergeant knew where the three men had gone and I had Sgt. Travis go and bring them in.

As a good many of the men were much the worse for liquor, I decided to march them all the way to Washington Barracks, three miles. At my request, the captain of police got a couple of firemen to accompany me, with buckets and wrenches for the hydrants, not only to furnish the men with drinking water, but to throw water over those who seemed to need a little bracing up. It was a terribly hot day, the first part of June, and when they arrived at the barracks, they were practically all sober. I halted them under the shade of the trees and gave them water, then reported their presence to the officer of the guard, who took charge of them.

I asked the First Sergeant why his men had acted the way they did. He told me the men were not particularly well disciplined, especially when officers were not present, and that their officers had gone on in parlor cars, paying no attention to them, and they had had practically nothing to eat for two days. When they saw the hotel across the street from the old Pennsylvania Station, he could not hold them. I asked him why they didn't obey the orders of the police and he said, "Lieutenant, my men are mainly Irish and they hate them shiners! But they will do anything you tell them to."

I had to make a written report about this, which Greely saw. It was composed in a very hasty manner, not well punc-

180

tuated, and I think perhaps some words were misspelled. General Greely sent for me and complimented me on handling the situation as well as I did, saying that I was about the same age as he was when he went into the service, eighteen years old. He then drew my attention to the report I had made and said, "Your report is a good one, it is short, concise, to the point and understandable. However, when reports are made, superior officers, often when they do not know their subordinates well, size them up according to the English used, the punctuation and the scholastic merit of the reports they make; and while I am not a stickler about correctness in these matters, I advise you always to be very careful in the preparation of any report." I have never forgotten these things and mention them here to show what great personal interest Greely took in every man under him.

General Greely, as head of the Signal Corps, was charged with acquiring and distributing military information. During the Spanish War, it devolved upon him to put censors over each submarine cable coming to the United States from foreign countries. He also arranged as far as possible with the foreign cable companies to send to the United States any information they might have about the movements of the Spanish fleet, which was then known to be on the way from Spain to Cuba. He soon found out that it had touched at the Cape Verde Islands and had left there on a certain date. He knew about how much coal they had and how long it would take them to get across the ocean, so ordered a strict watch on all cables. At Key West Lieut. Colonel Allen was the censor, and Signal men were put in as operators. There were Scotch operators at Havana, Cuba, with whom such pleasant relations were cultivated that Col. Allen got all the information he needed from Cuba, which he promptly relayed to Greely in Washington.

The question was raised as to whether submarine cables should be cut. Greely was summoned by President McKinley, before the full cabinet, to give them information on the cable situation. The question of the rights of neutral cable companies was brought up. Greely remarked that the Attorney-General, Griggs, was present and could tell them the law. The Attorney-General, taken by surprise, said that he had not studied the question. Greely then enumerated the various cable agreements, and the stipulation that neutral cables going into enemy countries could be cut at discretion within territorial waters. Submarine cables on the high seas that did not belong to the enemy could not be cut. Spain did not own any cables, but all neutral cables going to her territory were subject to the chances of war within a marine league of her coasts in Cuba and other possessions.

President McKinley then said to Greely, before the cabinet: "General, as the officer charged by law with the military means of communication, you are to assume charge of all cables and exercise such control over them and take such other action as is necessary to the public welfare and is legal." This direct order from the President to Greely put him in charge of all cables coming to the United States, and placed him directly under the orders of the President.

GENERAL A. W. GREELY
Chief Signal Officer, 1887-1906

Even with the experience of the Civil War behind them, the Army and Congress knew very little about electrical means of communication. The cable office under Colonel Allen was besieged by newspaper correspondents, Army and Navy officers, business men and dissatisfied cable officials asking for special privileges, but Allen held to his instructions and played no favorites. Some of these men went to the Secretary of War and persuaded him to close the office, claiming that keeping open the cables might be of advantage to the Spaniards; but Greely, knowing what a great advantage they were to us, recommended against it. Receiving an order for the second time from the Secretary of War to close the cable office, Greely answered, "You were present at the meeting of the Cabinet when the President vested me with sole and complete control of cables and their censorship. You must give me this order in writing and revoke my authority in the name of the President." This the Secretary of War refrained from doing. As a result, Greely took all confidential messages coming over the cables first to President McKinley.

While gossiping over the cable, Allen at Key West was informed that the Spanish fleet had left Martinique on May 11th. Greely had a little trouble in verifying this because the operator at Martinique, when called upon to confirm the matter, refused to have anything to do with an order coming from the direction of the United States. This was a French cable, and upon Greely's request, the cable authorities in France verified this for him. Greely had foreseen this and

183

made arrangements accordingly. It was found that the fleet called at Curaçao on May 14th and that Cervera arrived at Santiago on May 19th, with five ships, one ship arriving later. Before the last ship had gotten there, Allen was in possession of the facts in Key West. Immediately he sent the following message to Greely, in code: "Five Spanish vessels arrived at Santiago de Cuba. Have notified Admiral commanding (Sampson). The Spanish flagship arrived Santiago. The admiral (Cervera) hastily wired Madrid." Allen also gave this information to the senior naval officer at Key West.

Next morning Allen wired: "Pelayo and four cruisers in Santiago." General Greely at once took these messages in person to the President, who after listening to his report. said, "General, this news changes all our plans. Since Cervera is at Santiago, I will send for Secretary Long (Secretary of the Navy). Santiago must be blockaded at once." Heretofore Santiago had not been considered of much importance strategically and had not been blockaded. The official report of this incident was:

> The blockading of Cervera's squadron was due to the concerted action of the President and the Secretary of the Navy, based on reports and representations made to them personally by the Chief of the Signal Corps of the Army (General Greely).

The Santiago campaign was ordered and the army, under Shafter, assembled at Tampa for the attack on Havana, was diverted to that place. After this decision was reached, the Naval War Board informed the Secretary of the Navy that the Signal Corps had made a mistake and that Cervera was not at Santiago. The President sent for General Greely and said, "The Navy declares that your reports of Cervera's arrival at Santiago are incorrect."

"Where do they say Cervera is?" inquired Greely.

"They do not know for certain," answered the President, "but they insist he is not at Santiago. Now, General, you know that the plan of campaign was changed on your reports, which makes you responsible for it."

Greely answered that as he had been honored by the complete confidence of the President, he accepted the responsibility. He pointed out that every bit of information he had given the President heretofore had proved to be correct. McKinley acknowledged this and said he believed Greely was correct in this case, but he wished him to use his utmost endeavors to verify Cervera's presence in Santiago, not only from Havana but from other places. This Greely promised to do. Six cables led from Santiago to various places and Greely got confirmation from one or more of them every day.

He was returning to his office in the State, War and Navy Building after his interview with the President, when the Assistant Secretary of the Navy met him in the corridor and asked him into his office. After they entered, he locked the door and took Greely into a far corner of the room. "Your reports of the presence of Cervera's squadron in Santiago are not correct," he said. Greely asked, "Who gave you that information?" "The War Board," he answered. "Where does the War Board say the Spanish fleet is?" pursued Greely, to which the Secretary answered, "The War Board cannot locate it positively but declares it is not in Santiago Harbor." Greely, tired of these obstructionist tactics, said sarcastically that the War Board reminded him of the Three Wise Men who went to sea in a bowl and could not see beyond the rim; that it was the duty of the Navy to locate Cervera's squadron; the Navy did not know where it was but the Army did. Then he explained in detail why he knew the Spanish squadron was where it was, and ended the conversation.

The Navy was ordered to Santiago, but they did not verify the presence of Cervera's squadron until ten days after Greely had found it. Greely was therefore primarily responsible not only for the quick location of the Spanish fleet but also for the Santiago campaign which turned out to be one of the decisive military actions of history, and which ended the Spanish war.

Greely's labors did not stop there. General Shafter, commanding the Fifth Army Corps which was destined for the investment of Santiago, refused to have any field telegraph trains sent with the Corps. Greely sent them along anyway. He sent Colonel Allen on a foreign ship, because there were no American ships available, to cut the cables within three miles of Santiago Harbor. Allen's men fished these cables up under the direct fire of the Spanish batteries and cut them, with the crudest kind of equipment. This foreign ship sailed without a flag, without proper clearance papers, and might under some conditions have been regarded as a pirate.

Allen picked up the end of one of the cables, spliced it and landed the end at Guatanamo which had been seized by an advance party of marines; so when Shafter's army landed at Siboney for the Santiago campaign, messages could be sent to Washington within a few hours. This cable was later connected up to Shafter's headquarters by cable and field telegraph, so that he could talk direct to Washington. All this was done on Greely's initiative, as the old line officers with their bull-headed conservatism could not appreciate the necessity for it. Greely also sent a military balloon to Santiago, under a very capable officer who knew how to use it, but Shafter put an engineer officer over it who knew nothing about the handling of balloons, with the result that its work was very badly done, and instead of being a great advantage to the troops, it had much the opposite effect.

Although Greely was handicapped in the beginning by extremely limited funds and only a handful of personnel, he accomplished remarkable results. With his usual foresight, he appealed to the General Electric Company, Western Union and the Mexican Telegraph Company, who furnished him both expert telegraph operators and linemen and much material on credit.

On the completion of the Santiago campaign, Cuba was occupied by American forces. Telegraph lines had been torn up all over the island. In the latter part of 1898 we began the construction of a complete new telegraph system for

Cuba which was finished the following spring. I had the honor of completing the telegraph lines through Santiago Province, now called Oriente, in the eastern part of Cuba. It was pioneer work of an entirely new kind to the American soldiers. We had to vary our methods to fit conditions in a tropical country, with strange people to deal with, a strange language (which we soon learned) and strange diseases, among them the dreaded yellow fever.

Chapter XV

PHILIPPINE CAMPAIGN—ALASKAN DUTY

NO sooner had our labors in Cuba been completed than the insurrection in the Philippine Islands burst furiously into flames, in the spring of 1899. This insurrection had been well organized under General Emilio Aguinaldo, a man of great political and military ability. Insurgent forces took the field in every inhabited island in the archipelago. Forty thousand well armed, well disciplined and well instructed Philippine troops faced our small forces in Manila and vicinity. The insurgents were provided with infantry, cavalry and artillery. They had repaired the telegraph lines formerly used by the Spanish for their own communications.

An offensive campaign was decided upon, and reënforcements sent to General Otis, then commanding. I immediately applied for that duty and was sent there. The problem was above all one of rapid communication because the insurgents, knowing the country, having friends everywhere, could scatter and reassemble with the greatest ease. It took quick action to get in contact with them. The Chief Signal Officer of the army in Manila asked for 100 miles of telegraph wire. Greely sent him 1000 miles. Even this revision of the estimate fell short of their needs, because eventually 16,000 miles of wire and cables were laid in the Philippines.

Whenever a column moved, we had to keep in touch with them with a field telegraph line. I remember once in the northern advance in the fall of 1899, when we attempted to capture Aguinaldo's army by surrounding him with three columns, one under General MacArthur, one under General Lawton and the third under General Wheaton. Communication with General Lawton failed, because his Signal Corps detachments could not keep up with him. We had not heard from him for several days and it became imperative to get into communication with him. Our column, MacArthur's, was at a place called Bautista, and we figured that Lawton must have arrived at or near a town called Tayug, some 70 or 80 miles way. The country was full of insurgents. Mounted patrols had not been able to push through. MacArthur called his Chief of Signal Corps, Captain Carr, and asked him what he could do. When I heard of it, I volunteered to go through. There were twelve men I could take, splendid fellows. We had few telegraph instruments, only keys and relays, no batteries, wires or insulators. Carr asked, "What can you do without these things?"

I had found some insurgent wire-wound cannon, captured when we attacked Bautista, and we unwound this wire; also we discovered many rolls of barbed wire, used for entanglements, and some old Spanish Leclanché batteries; but we had no sal ammoniac to put them in. I decided to try ordinary table or rock salt, and found that it produced a current but it was so weak that often we could only detect it by touching our tongues to the wire and putting a hand in a muddy place on the earth, for a ground. However, we could read the dots and dashes. We had no transportation but I succeeded in seizing about twenty water buffalo, carabao they are called, and made pack saddles for them out of dried banana leaves and stalks and manila hemp. All this was done in the space of a few hours, with our men and a few loyal natives working night and day.

I started with the detachment for General Lawton, with the blessings of our comrades who never expected to see us again. Luck was with us and our line worked, with wire from the wire-wound guns, barbed wire, fence wire, insulators made of dried bamboo and pieces of bottles. We worked night and day, with insurgent forces retreating all around us, pouring out through a hole between Lawton's and Wheaton's columns that had not been filled due to lack of communication. A running fight was kept up nearly all the time, but fortunately none of my men was killed. As the insurgents fell back, they barbarously killed the people they thought were opposed to them, disemboweling some and tearing them all to pieces. In one place I ran into a few Spaniards who had been held prisoners. They thought their hour had come. I have never seen men more scared, and until one has seen men in mortal fear, it is impossible to visualize their condition. They can hardly talk or even stand erect. They hide behind any little thing that offers the slightest cover and will not move except at night and then in the stealthiest way. I could not do much for these poor fellows, so turned them over to a Philippine priest who had a church in the town and told him to take care of them. If any harm befell them, I promised that on my return I would kill him and burn everything he had. He promised to care for them, and did so.

As we had no means of protecting our line behind us, I let it be known everywhere we saw natives that if the wire was molested in any way, or if it was cut and not repaired at once, that the houses for two miles on each side of the road would be burned and all the cattle and horses killed. It was cut in a couple of places by retreating insurgents but immediately repaired by the inhabitants.

At 2 o'clock in the morning, we hit Lawton's outposts and went straight into the town of Tayug with our wire. Lawton was quartered in a convent with his adjutant-general, later Major-General Clarence Edwards, and his aides, the present Major-General E. L. King, and Lieut. Sewell of New Jersey, since resigned from the service. As we finished connecting the lines, we were so tired we did not care much what we encountered that was suitable for a telegraph pole. A large cross was standing in front of Lawton's headquarters in the convent. To my horror next day I found that we had nailed an insulator to the face of it to bring the wire into headquarters.

Fifteen minutes after we arrived, we had the telegraph line working. Lawton would not believe it until he came down and saw the instruments. After two or three hours' rest, I had the doctors look over the wounds of my men. As their clothing was in rags and they were practically barefooted, I tried to get some clothing. Lieut. King had captured a store of old Spanish uniforms and they were the only garments we could get. Of course if we wore them we might be mistaken for insurgents and shot, but we took them anyhow, turned them wrong side out and put them on. We started back without escort or any other help, repairing the line as we went. I mention this to show what we were up against in this campaign. Men of the Signal Corps went all over the enemy country, laying their lines, against as great obstacles as have ever been encountered in a tropical campaign.

With General MacArthur's headquarters there were only two signal officers, Captain Carr and myself, but communication never failed them. Training of this sort was the greatest possible education to younger officers in self-reliance, resourcefulness and perseverance. Greely was responsible for this sort of spirit, not only because he had selected the personnel himself, but also because whenever work was gone at with a will and in a proper way, no matter what the results, he always stood behind his men, and we knew it. He planned and supervised the construction of all military telegraph and cable lines in the Philippines, and later made a personal inspection of all the work.

Largely due to this communication system, within a year the Philippine Islands were pacified. This labyrinth of 2000 islands and islets, with fifty-two written and spoken languages, formed one of the most difficult problems that any army ever tackled. I doubt if any troops other than Americans could have done it. When I say this, I am familiar with the troops of all the great nations of the world.

From the Philippines, the Signal Corps accompanied the column for the relief of the legations in Peking in 1900. It was the only organization that carried a wire up to the gates of Peking during the assault. Within a couple of hours after the city was taken, Captain Stamford of the Signal Corps announced to the world that the legations were relieved and our diplomatic agents saved.

The next work of the Signal Corps was the construction of the Alaska telegraph and cable system. Up to that time it had been considered that the difficulties of building a telegraph line in Alaska were insurmountable. In the fifties and sixties, the Western Union company had attempted to cut a right of way up to Bering Strait and thus establish telegraphic communication with Europe via Siberia, but the project had resulted in dismal failure. About that time, 1868, the first Atlantic cable was laid by Cyrus W. Field, which made it unnecessary to complete the Alaskan telegraph line.

With the great rush of prospectors to the gold fields in Alaska, and the Klondike in Canada just across from our frontier, came the necessity for establishing a number of army posts in that area. The question of building lines of communication was broached to Greely and he said he could do it. He submitted an estimate amounting to a little over $1,000,000 for this stupendous work. Knowing what Arctic conditions in Alaska were, he was more familiar with what could be done than any one else in the service. Officers and men from the line of the army, that is, the infantry, had made a failure of it; so as soon as a few Signal Corps officers could be gathered up, they were sent to take charge of it. I volunteered and took a detachment to Alaska via the White Pass, then down the Yukon River in a flatboat to Eagle City, where we established our base.

To make a long story short, we completed the Alaska telegraph system, some 2200 miles, within two years, over trackless Arctic wastes, working winter and summer. During the last winter, we worked through temperatures under 60 below zero, for six weeks, our coldest recorded weather being 76 below zero. It is one of the coldest parts of the world. In the summer we had to wade through the deep moss and marshy ground which extended to the hilltops, scourged by the terrible mosquitoes and black flies which made the men's faces and hands running sores, and drove our pack animals to frenzy. Although some outstanding trips had been made through Alaska, it had never been reconnoitered thoroughly except along certain of the most easily traveled routes. Our lines opened Alaska up to civilization. In addition to planning these lines, General Greely made trips of inspection through the entire territory, visiting every station.

When the line was finally completed, there was no way of getting messages to the United States except by boat from Prince William Sound. The Canadians had built a telegraph line to Dawson City, Y. T., within 121 miles of Eagle City, Alaska. At that time the Canadian and American governments had some very unpleasant questions to settle relating to the frontier and the gold mining districts. The American government did not wish to ask any favors from Canada. However, Sir Wilfrid Laurier, then Premier, was a close personal friend of Greely's. Greely asked the President to allow him on his own responsibility to go and see his friend, Premier Laurier, and talk the matter over with him. Permission was granted on the basis that it would be entirely a personal matter with Greely, and the United States would take no responsibility in the matter. In case he failed, it would be to his own detriment. Greely went to Ottawa, saw Laurier, showed him that it would be a good financial proposition for the Canadians to handle all our telegraph business from Alaska and would undoubtedly tend to renew our former amicable relations. Laurier agreed to build the line from Dawson City to the border, for which an appropriation of $30,000 was immediately made by the Canadian Parliament. It was built at once and through telegraphic communication established.

In 1901, the Signal Corps installed the world's first commercial long distance wireless telegraph system, under Capt. Leonard Wildman. It extended from St. Michael, Alaska, to Nome, across Norton Sound.

It soon became evident that with the growing controversy over boundaries between Canada and the United States, it was not desirable to have all messages sent from Alaska pass through the hands of Canadian officials. In case any real trouble occurred, the lines through Canada might not be available to Alaska. Mr. Root, then Secretary of War, talked over with General Greely the matter of establishing a cable from Puget Sound to Alaska. He was afraid that if it were known we contemplated laying this cable, it might add fuel to Canada's resentment. Greely told him he could arrange matters so that no mention of a cable would be made until it was laid, and the next morning had prepared an estimate for connecting the military district at St. Michael with the military department of Columbia at Seattle, Washington.

He then went to "Uncle Joe" Cannon of the Committee of Appropriations of the House of Representatives, explained what the project was about and asked him to keep it quiet. The appropriation was made and Congress adjourned next day. No notice appeared about it in any newspaper. If Greely had ordered the Continental gutta-percha cable in Europe, the cat might have been out of the bag, as it would have been suspected what the cable was for. Gutta-percha cable could not be made in the United States at that time. Greely contracted for an American cable with rubber insulation, although this type of insulation had never been used with success before.

The cable ship *Burnside* was brought across the Pacific from Manila "for repairs." Greely sent the rubber cable across the United States by train, to be put in the cable ship at Seattle, against the advice of his technical men, who thought the cable would be injured. European cable experts prophesied that this cable would not work, but it was laid from Seattle to Juneau and Skagway, then to Valdez,

Alaska. It was guaranteed to last for ten years but demonstrated that it could last at least three times that long. It was laid under very difficult conditions over uncharted seas, on a sea bed that is one of the roughest in the world, and exposed to some of the fastest tides and currents. The work was under Colonel Allen and Captain Russell, with Captain Chandler in command of the cable ship. More than 3000 miles of cable were laid and regularly operated, sufficient to connect America with Europe. At that time there was in operation in Alaska a Signal Corps system of radio, telegraph and cables nearly 5000 miles long.

Chapter XVI

FIRST AIRPLANE—FIRST RADIO—LAST INDIAN UPRISING

GREELY, with his active mind always searching with prophetic foresight for things that would benefit this country, kept in close touch with Professor Langley and his experiments with mechanical flight. Charged as the Chief of Signal Corps was with handling balloons and aerial matters, Greely was thoroughly alive to the benefits that could accrue from navigation of the air. People were laughing at things of that kind then. Professor Simon Newcomb had proved, to his own satisfaction at least, that mechanical flight was not possible, but Greely knew that it was.

In 1898, Congress appropriated $50,000 for the construction of a flying machine for war purposes and Greely was charged with the duty of expending this money. Others had refused to handle it as they thought it was doomed to ridicule and failure. Greely had always expended his utmost efforts toward securing aid for Langley, whose experiments had been made in secret. Greely knew he had built what was called an airdrome, really an airplane equipped with a steam engine, which had made flights through free air of from half a mile to a mile, but it was not large enough to carry much weight. The perfection of a man-carrying machine was only an extension of this problem. Greely's comments in requesting this appropriation of $50,000 show remarkable foresight, in the light of the subsequent development of the flying machine. In his letter to the Secretary of War, he said, "Professor Langley's public spirit has been shown by his declination to take out patents, and the great importance of such a machine for warfare and the great good that would result to the world at large should the flying machine be made practicable, are cogent reasons for favorable action."

This is what really led to our conquest of the air. Even then it was with the greatest difficulty that Greely persuaded Langley to undertake the work. Langley hesitated to do it because he considered that he had not many years to live, that he had great international standing as a scientist which he did not wish to impair by a possible failure, and that if he took up the building of this flying machine, it would mean the abandonment of his comfortable life as an individual. He felt that he had already demonstrated the soundness of his theories, in his smaller airdromes, and was willing that some one else should carry on the work where he left off. He told General Greely that he knew men could fly, but the thing that bothered him was making a landing when going forty miles an hour, so as not to destroy the machine or kill the pilot. While he was sure of ultimate success, he was afraid that some slight failure might bring about a great deal of criticism that would embitter his life and cause him to be held up to the ridicule of the press, which he could not endure.

However, he finally acceded to Greely's request and built the man-carrying Langley airdrome. The machine was perfectly capable of flying but some small accidents prevented a completely successful demonstration. In the final attempt to fly the airdrome on Dec. 8, 1903, a defect in the launching gear resulted in the breaking up of the machine and the ending of the experiment. As Langley had foreseen, the ridicule of the press was heaped on him and it had a great deal to do with his early end, as he was a very sensitive man.

The basis for the heavier-than-air flying machine had been laid and the Wright brothers who first flew said of Langley, "The knowledge that the head of the most prominent scientific institution of America believed in the possibility of human flight was one of the influences that led us to undertake the preliminary investigations that preceded our active work. He recommended to us the books that enabled us to form sound ideas at the outset. It was a helping hand at a critical time and we shall always be grateful."

Greely not only was a moving spirit behind the development of our first flying machines, but he inculcated into all of us in his Corps the feeling that some day we would navigate the air. Even while engaged in the construction of telegraph lines in Arctic Alaska in 1901, I was studying assiduously the development and handling of lighter-than-air craft, kites and gliders, and it served me in good stead, not only when I first took up aviation in earnest but when I commanded and later developed our aviation, up to the present time.

Greely assembled and developed the War Department

Library, which had not amounted to much before his magic hand touched it. This saved the remarkable Brady Civil War photographs. A compilation of literature about the Civil War was also arranged and made available for the use of officers and educational institutions. It was about this time, too, that he started the first Free Public Library in Washington, by personally soliciting funds and private subscriptions for it. He received a good-sized contribution from the owner of one of the city's newspapers. Later, this gentleman telephoned to General Greely, saying he would double the size of his contribution if Greely would withdraw his name as sponsor of the fund and permit the publisher's son's name to be used instead, an offer which General Greely declined.

In 1903, Greely was sent to the first International Wireless Conference in Berlin, at which nine nations were represented, and where international radio regulations were formulated for the first time. The old line people in the army laughed at radio then, but Greely could see its great future.

In that same year, Company "A" of the Signal Corps under my command formed the first field radio stations, carried on pack mules. The following year, with wire raised on kites about two miles in the air, I took a radio message over the longest distance yet received, at Fort Leavenworth, Kansas, from the Steamer *Navarisk* that was entering San Juan Harbor, about 1900 miles away. The next night we took one from the Steamer *Concho*, which was leaving Key West, Florida. Although three decades have passed, I remember very distinctly hearing the words come in over the electrolytic detector from the *Concho*. The signals were slow and heavy and at a rather low key. The radiogram was addressed to "Miss Mamie Fisher, 408 San Joaquin Street, Houston, Texas." As her name was pronounced, a lieutenant standing beside me, named Olney Place, exclaimed, "Why, I have known that young lady for many years."

Representatives of the press who were present were greatly astonished, not only that messages could be received for that long distance totally without wires, but that there was so little privacy about them. Anybody fishing around in the air for these radio impulses could pick them up. It led to quite a good deal of controversy in the press. The scoffers and doubters had to acknowledge that there was something to radio telegraphy, after all.

By the efforts of the Signal Corps under General Greely's direction, military radio, or wireless communication as we called it then, was advanced further than that of any other nation, as were other forms of military signaling.

At the beginning of the Spanish War, Greely had declined a Major Generalship, because its acceptance would have meant his being transferred out of the Signal Corps, and he knew he could do more for his country in the Signal Corps than in any other organization. After the war, when his name came up again for appointment as Major General and he felt he could leave the Corps, he heard that he was going to be skipped over again. He went to see President Roosevelt about it, who said that two other people were being considered for the promotion, and that he had had some very influential letters from their friends. Frederick Dent Grant, the son of General U. S. Grant, was one of the men. "Well," General Greely said, "if that is the way you make appointments, I won't be appointed." He felt that unless the merit of his services justified it, and was made the basis for the promotion, he would not wish to accept it. He would never bring political pressure to bear to accomplish a thing of that kind.

However, on February 10, 1906, General Greely was promoted to be a Major-General in the line of the Army. He was assigned to the command of the Pacific Division, with headquarters at San Francisco. No sooner had he become settled in the duties of his new post than the terrible earthquake and fire occurred, on April 18, 1906. General Greely was away from the city when the earthquake occurred, in Chicago, on the way to Washington for his daughter's wedding. The catastrophe was so appalling that the civil authorities were completely paralyzed, incapable of doing anything. General Funston, second in command and in charge during General Greely's absence, immediately occupied the city with United States troops. There was no legal authority whatever for doing this, but the law of necessity and humanity dictated the action. When Greely heard about the disaster, he telegraphed the Secretary of War that he was returning to his post. Secretary Taft wired back that there was no necessity for an immediate return, but Greely replied that in time of national emergency, he would not be absent from duty. He took the first train going west and rejoined his post.

General Greely again demonstrated his profound knowledge of organization and the handling of people, and ably seconded by General Funston, put a plan into operation at once for the relief, feeding and care of this great multitude. The city was still in flames. Houses were being blown up to stop the spread of the fire. The streets in the lower part of the city were a terrible mass of wreckage, through which a way had to be blown with dynamite. Hundreds of people were dead, the exact number will never be known. More than 200,000 were homeless and without food.

All lines of transportation and communication had been destroyed or interrupted. There was not even a direct telegraph wire out of San Francisco. The water system was all broken up. Smallpox and typhoid fever were present and it was feared a general pestilence would result. Even when rations were issued to the people, they could not cook in their houses as chimneys and walls had been knocked down. They had to make fires in the streets and live in little wickiups wherever they could get a corner and a few boards to shelter them.

I had the only organized signal company in the army at that time, stationed at Fort Leavenworth, Kansas. I received orders on the morning of the catastrophe to proceed to San Francisco immediately. We were loaded on a special train and reached there on the third day. We went to work right away and established communication all over the city and with the outside world. The cables of the street railway, inoperative at the time, were hitched up to "buzzers" by the Signal Corps and communication along them established.

Troops were stationed at key points and patrols established to prevent looting and stealing and to insure safety. Instructions were issued as to the rules of conduct every one should follow. Each person was given a card of identification, which also stated what he was entitled to from the relief stores. Food and clothing sent in from all parts of the country were distributed. Six relief districts were established, the largest of which I was put in charge of. Soup kitchens were set up, and shelters provided.

Some looting of food trucks and wagons was going on, and General Greely ordered that an armed soldier accompany each truck, with instructions to shoot if anything was touched. Mayor Rolph of San Francisco and a group of prominent citizens who had called on Greely for aid, protested at this saying, "You can't do that. The food belongs to the people of San Francisco." "No," answered General Greely, "it belongs to the *distressed* people of San Francisco and it is my place to say who is distressed." One of the men said, "Some one will be shot!" General Greely replied, "Gentlemen, when the first man is shot, come to me and I will consider rescinding the order." From the moment armed soldiers were put on the trucks, there was no further looting and no casualties.

The citizens, though stunned by the disaster, coöperated manfully with the troops when shown what to do. It was a revelation to me to see men who were masters of business and captains of industry utterly at a loss and incapable of any initiative in such a terrible emergency; and it was equally interesting to see how the officers of the military service, from second lieutenant up, who were trained to act definitely and quickly in emergencies, did exactly the right thing under the most trying and difficult circumstances.

At one place in the lower part of my district, the building of the California Wine Company had been completely burned down, and the great wooden wine casks with it. The wine had spilled down into the concrete cellar where it remained, to a depth of several feet. The tough characters from the Barbary Coast near by discovered this. They took buckets to which they attached ropes, dipped up the wine from the cellar pool and passed it around. Soon there was a horde of dangerous drunks, and it looked as if a riot would ensue which could not be quelled without much loss of life. However, the regular troops restored order without killing a man, and placed a guard over the cellar. The wine was pumped out by the Fire Department into lighters which carried it across San Francisco Bay, and it was subsequently made into brandy.

All saloons and liquor dispensing establishments were closed and the stocks of spirits, taken over by the military authorities, were placed under guard. In some instances men buried their liquor, to hide it from the authorities, digging it up at night and selling it. We adopted a system of detectives among the civilian population which soon located these caches and confiscated them.

Sanitary conditions had to be looked after most carefully, but under the direction of the Army surgeons disease and epidemics were kept under control.

In the face of adversity, the bravery of the people was wonderful. General Greely said that throughout the disaster he never heard a man complain or saw a woman weep. They looked with dry eyes at their wrecked and ruined houses where their life savings had been invested, and began to clear away the débris so as to erect another home. I saw only one instance of people completely losing their self-control and that was when the fine houses along Van Ness Avenue, one of the best residence districts of the city, had to be blown up to stop the spread of the flames. The owners could not understand why their houses, removed several blocks from the actual conflagration, should be dynamited with everything in them. Many of these people had to be restrained by force and taken away. But it was this very thing that stopped the spread of the flames in that direction. It does no good to blow up a house that is already on fire. That merely spreads it. A real fireproof space must be provided across which a fire cannot go.

A fire that has gotten out of control is a terrible thing. The San Francisco fire was the worst we have ever had in America, and up to that time probably the worst that had ever occurred. The heat from this conflagration crumbled the front of buildings several blocks away, particularly those made of granite, and it was an awe-inspiring sight to see the front of a building not on fire suddenly slide down and collapse. In some places, the fire was so intense that all the oxygen in the air was used up. Gases would form that only needed oxygen to cause combustion. These gases, invisible of course, would roll down the streets until several blocks away from the actual fire, when they would unite with the necessary oxygen and flames would spring up, setting a new section afire. For awhile it was thought that incendiaries were causing these fires, but similar occurrences have been noted in all big conflagrations. In the Great London Fire of 1666, when conflagrations were not well understood, the people thought that the devil was putting fire balls in the church steeples several blocks away from the actual fire.

Gradually the people regained their composure. Lines of transportation and communication were repaired, largely under the guidance of the Army. After a month, certain restrictions were put on the issuance of food so as to make the people go back to work, first one article and then another being cut out of the allowance. The largest falling off in applications for rations occurred when coffee and sugar were eliminated. After the first month, the feeding was done by contract, and temporary buildings erected where eligible refugees came and had regular meals. There was no distinction as to class, race or religion. All had to sit together to get their food. A woman complained to General Greely that she was forced to eat at the same table with a negro. "Doubtless they are hungry," General Greely replied gravely, but with the suggestion of a twinkle in his eye. "The negro who sat next to me as I took my luncheon yesterday ate enormously." There seemed to be no suitable grounds for further complaint after this innocent observation, so the conversation ended.

The number of applicants for relief eventually dwindled to about 15,000, the average number of beggars, unemployed and people who will not work in normal times. While many supplies were contributed from various parts of the United States, it was really California that looked after its own people, reassuring evidence that the pioneer spirit still remained among them.

Greely worked consistently to put all the civil authorities back on the job, and by July 1st the Army had relinquished its control over the civil population. At the very beginning, William H. Taft, then Secretary of War, had entrusted the handling of everything in San Francisco to General Greely. Although martial law had never been declared and the Army acted entirely on the initiative of its own officers, no trouble of any kind grew out of it, no claims for the destruction of property or the detention of individuals. This disaster brought together the largest force of the Army, Navy and Marine Corps that had ever worked together in time of peace. The way they handled the situation was a monument to the devotion and discipline of the troops and the wisdom and ability of their commanding officer, General Greely. During the Army's administration, there had been no murders, riots, epidemics or formal criticism, and all deserving persons applying were given food and clothing. It was a remarkable demonstration of the use of a trained and organized force in time of emergency.

General Greely, in his capacity as Commanding General of the Northern Military Division, was called upon to handle the last Indian campaign in the West. In 1905, the Ute Indians, numbering about 400, claimed that they were illtreated and abandoned their reservation in Utah and marched into Wyoming. The people were fearful that the usual outrages incident to an Indian invasion would occur. The governor of Wyoming, under the provisions of the Constitution, called on the Federal government for help. The President directed General Greely, specifically, to take charge of the situation.

Greely was familiar with the character of the Utes and knew the country intimately through which they were traveling, where the white settlers were, and where the United States troops were stationed. If fighting started, he knew it would lead to a wholesale murder of men, women and children, so he laid his plans to avoid it. He placed a company of scouts on the trail of the Utes, who kept a constant surveillance over them but did not come into actual contact with them. He then stationed troops at various key points so as to completely surround the Indians. Before long, the Indians entrenched themselves, thinking they were going to be attacked; whereupon Greely began to parley with them.

He let them know what troops he had available, where they were stationed and what he would do in case the Utes did not abide by the conditions he laid down. Seeing the utter futility of any resistance, the Indians agreed to keep quiet for a year if he would send them to a certain reservation. This Greely did, and the Indians stood by their word, giving no further trouble. Not an Indian was killed or a settler injured in any way. It probably was the best solution to an Indian problem ever worked out in this country.

Chapter XVII

MAJOR-GENERAL, RETIRED

IT was while he was in command of the Pacific Division, in 1908, that the time drew near for General Greely's retirement from active service. At the age of 64 he was hale, hearty and at the height of his mental vigor. Mrs. Greely, with her usual wise foresight, knew there would be a great gap to bridge; he was so active that he would be very unhappy when he retired, unless he had something to absorb his interest and energy. She decided they must make a trip around the world, she and General Greely and two of their daughters, Rose and Gertrude.

The month of March found them on the high seas, bound for the Philippines, where they visited for awhile. Then in a leisurely fashion they saw Japan, where they were entertained by Minister of the Navy Saito, at an old-time feast attended by distinguished guests of the samurai class. This was the same Saito who, as Naval Attaché in the United States, had greeted General Greely at Portsmouth in 1884, on his return from the Arctic. Saito afterward became Governor General of Korea, then Premier of Japan.

From Japan they went on to China. General Greely had been through the Suez Canal several times, but had not seen Asiatic Russia, so it was decided to go to Europe via the

213

Trans-Siberian Railway. Taking the train at Vladivostok, they were eleven or twelve days crossing Siberia. Its vast plains and rugged mountains reminded them of the western United States. At the larger towns, their train would stop for an hour or so, for the chef to do his marketing, and the Greelys took these opportunities to walk around and see the sights. At little way stations, when the engine took on fuel, they got out and picked flowers. When the engineer was ready to proceed, he tooted his whistle two or three times for them to return.

At Moscow they took the train for Berlin, and spent some time in Germany, mostly in Dresden. In the fall they went on down to Italy, making Florence their headquarters for the winter. A cousin of Mrs. Greely's, who had married an Italian nobleman, had a villa in Florence and introduced them to local society. Besides the active social life they led, each of the Greelys studied something: Gertrude was in school, Rose took courses in metal repoussé work and history of art, and General Greely took up bookbinding, in which he became much interested. From time to time they made a great many little trips, to the Austrian Tyrol, and motored through the northern Italian hill towns with friends from home whom they chanced to meet.

Late in 1909 they returned to America, to their house in Washington on G Street, between 19th and 20th, one of the oldest residential sections of the city, about two blocks from the State, War and Navy Building. The house had an old-fashioned dignity and grace, with its high ceilings and formal arrangements, and was made doubly charming by Mrs. Greely's good taste. Although the income of the Greely family was never large, nothing seemed to be lacking in the way of comforts. Once when I passed through Washington between a change of stations, in 1904, General Greely turned the house over to me, the family being away.

The family life of the Greelys was outstandingly happy. As one intimate friend describes it:

"It was like nothing else I have ever known. After all, they were all so original, so individual, that you wouldn't expect them to have an ordinary family life. They usually congregated in the library where General Greely was working, and although they all talked at once, he did not seem to be disturbed, but wrote busily on. Tea would be brought in and served, he would stop a few minutes and drink a cup with them, then resume his work amid the soaring conversation."

There were six children: Antoinette, Adola, Rose and Gertrude were the girls, John and Adolphus Jr. (Dolph) the boys. Adola, the beauty of the family, was one of twins, the other having died in infancy. Rose was distinguished by her artistic ability. There was a depth and appeal to the poetry she used to write that made it quite unusual. Later she turned this creative impulse in another direction, and is now a well-known and successful landscape architect.

But talented, charming and beautiful as the daughters were, none of them, in the opinion of the friend just quoted, could touch their mother for looks and social graces.

"She was one in a million. Born abroad of American par-

215

ents, she had all the grace of a foreigner. She was tall and graceful, aristocratic and gracious. She used to be quite intimate with Mrs. Grover Cleveland, who was supposed to be quite a beauty, but I can tell you that Mrs. Greely was much the handsomer of the two. And it was not only her looks, but her interest in people as well, that constituted her unique charm. If anything was going on in Washington, she got invitations for you and arranged for you to go. She didn't wait to ask if you wanted to.

"She was, one might say, worldly-minded, in the best sense of the word. She loved the frills of life! I remember she dressed in a distinguished way on nothing at all. Her family, the Nesmiths, had once had a great deal of money and property, but lost much of it in the Civil War. She still had some land in California, and I think whenever crises came up, about how to educate John, for instance, she would sell a few lots in San Diego, and John would go to Yale!

"She never compromised or allowed herself to deviate from the standards she had set herself. At the same time, she was tolerant and broad minded. For instance, she had decided opinions on the subject of divorce, but she never tried to impose her views on any of her friends. In fact, two of her closest friends were divorcées. When taxed with inconsistency, she replied that she was not responsible for her friends' morals, only for her own and those she should instill in her children.

"I once asked General Greely, 'General, did you ever

216

think that Mrs. Greely was unusual, or did you just take her for granted, as a matter of course?'

" 'Oh, no,' was his reply, 'I always knew she was unusual.' "

For years the Greelys kept a coupé and a gray horse, named "Fleet," even after automobiles became quite common. Mrs. Greely distrusted motor cars quite strongly, and never wanted to go over eighteen miles an hour in them. When she got ready to pay some calls, the butler changed his costume to that of a coachman, and drove her round. Once or twice they took Fleet with them to New Hampshire for the summer, and it was there he spent his last days.

Their summer home was at Conway, New Hampshire, where they first started going in the early nineteen hundreds. Mrs. Greely's cousin, Joe Nesmith, an artist, had discovered the place and bought up seven or eight miles along the front of Lake Pequaquet (now called Conway Lake). He thought it the most beautiful place in the world, and painted a great deal there. At first the Greelys rented a cottage on the lake from Cousin Joe, which they called "White Birches." In 1912 or 1913, Rose and Gertrude bought an old abandoned farmhouse, about eight miles from South Conway, which they named "Hidden House." It is what its name implies, rather difficult to find. A newspaper reporter once spent three days driving around the country trying to find it, when General Greely's opinion was being sought during the Peary-Cook controversy. He went back to Boston unsuccessful, and stated that the North Pole was easier to find than General Greely.

The road that winds along the lake front makes a sharp hairpin turn after several miles, and there if you have sharp eyes you will see a tiny sign, "General Greely, 150 yards."

The house is a low, rambling one and a half story white clapboard structure, very typical of that part of the country. The rooms are small, with very low ceilings. The big barn is hitched on to the house by a connecting woodshed, two walls of which have been removed so that it serves as a porch. That is the way most New Hampshire farmhouses are built, with everything under one roof for the winter.

They did very little to change the house, but added a small lean-to room for General Greely, which he called his office. It was built of old boards from a barn and left quite plain. Austere and unaffected, it was a real explorer's room, not the sort designed by interior decorators with pine paneling and every refinement, but what an explorer would make for himself. The walls were lined with bookshelves from floor to ceiling, crammed with books and papers and orderly litter. In front of the west window was a high window seat, one of the distinctive features of any house General Greely lived in. There was one in the living room also, to catch the morning sun. They were much too high for the ordinary person but just right for General Greely, who was so tall. He liked to sit on them with his feet drawn up, enjoying the sunshine. They had no spring cushions or soft pillows on them, merely a straight pad to cover the hard boards. The family called them "Father's shelves." As he grew older, he often sat there all afternoon, and during his last years if you happened to call at the house, you would find General Greely sitting on one of his "shelves."

The window commanded a splendid view of the White Mountains, particularly Moat and Chocoroa Mountains. These are Indian names, Chocoroa being named after a famous Indian chief of that region. General Greely thought Moat had the most beautiful line of any mountain in the world. It was not high but long, and looked like an old Indian lying down, very peaceful and serene.

The country round about was natural and unspoiled. Lake, woodland and mountains were all beautiful, and ideal for a summer residence. Most of the farms near by had been deserted as conditions of life in the winter are so harsh and the land so unproductive. There were a few "summer people" here and there, but Conway has never been "discovered" or made fashionable, so it is uncrowded, remote, like a world unto itself.

General Greely used to walk a good deal, up to the last three or four years, but he had to have some objective, it was no aimless "walk." Usually he called at the Bairds', who lived about a mile distant, uphill all the way. He walked very slowly and picked flowers as he went along. When he arrived, he would present the bouquet to Mrs. Baird, saying, "Here is your daily present." If it was not flowers, it would be something unusual he had picked up in the woods.

Bishop Brewster of Connecticut used to visit him. It was

delightful to see the two distinguished looking old gentlemen going out to pick blackberries, blueberries or wild strawberries. One would meet them along the road with their berry pails and little stools, carrying on the most erudite and abstruse conversation; then they would stop to compare how much they had picked!

General Greely's tastes were very simple. He combined in an unusual way simplicity and dignity. He was at home in any company. He was one of the greatest men I ever knew, a real philosopher, greatest in his acceptance of life and the way he lived it. He never complained and no one knew when he made an effort. He had tremendous fortitude. He was never nervous and never made other people nervous. You hardly knew he had a body. When he was ill, you might know he was suffering, but he never had that attitude of some one grinning and bearing it. He did not struggle uselessly.

He seemed to have no interest in possessions or comforts. After his death, when his daughters wished to give some intimate possession of his to a cousin, an elderly lady of whom he had been quite fond, they could find nothing suitable, outside his books, except a little Sèvres after-dinner coffee cup that he had bought in France before he was married, which he still used daily up to his last illness.

He had no fanaticism, and he had no mean or little ways or thoughts. No one ever heard him say a mean thing about another person. He was incapable of it. He was deeply religious in his own way, but he had no dogmatic beliefs. His answer to the riddle of the universe was "I don't know," but he lived his life according to Christian principles.

He believed he owed his perfect health to moderation. He never ate very much. On the doctor's orders, he drank a gill of wine every day, usually with his lunch. He used to say that he abandoned smoking when he was eight years old, because his mother persuaded him it was not a wise habit. A rugged constitution and independent spirit characterized his old age. He was 87 when he suddenly decided that his teeth were giving him too much trouble and must go. He announced that he was going to the dispensary and have them all pulled out. His daughter Rose, who lived with him, was in bed with a broken arm, and tried to dissuade him, but quite unsuccessfully. He would not even take a taxi, but insisted on going alone by street car. As soon as he was out of the house, Rose telephoned a cousin, explaining the situation and asking her to drop by the dispensary and see General Greely home. The cousin, knowing that the old General hated to feel he was the object of care, waited until he emerged from the doorway and was standing on the corner waiting for the street car. Then she drove up as though by chance and hailed him, asking if she could give him a lift anywhere. General Greely, looking a little strange and shaky, accepted and climbed in the car, but it was his victory, he had not given in to any undignified coddling.

*   *   *   *   *

It was in 1911 that he was recalled by the President to active service and sent to represent the American Army at the coronation of George V of Great Britain. He went to this great display of pomp and pageantry directly from the Spartan simplicity of "Hidden House."

It was the occasion for many pleasant reunions with people he had known from all over the world and for forming new friendships with leaders in world thought and politics who had come together for that function.

The former British military attaché to the United States acted as General Greely's aide, and one day he said, "I suppose you will be wanting to see about your knee breeches for the Coronation."

General Greely replied that he would just as soon wear civilian clothes with knee breeches, or the full dress American army uniform with no knee breeches, as the regulations for the uniform did not prescribe them. There was a good deal of discussion about the matter, but at last General Greely received word to wear the full dress American Army uniform without knee breeches. Admiral Vreeland, representing the United States Navy, had ordered knee breeches to wear with his uniform, so General Greely was the only man there without knee breeches, and it was widely commented on.

About a week later, he was invited to a dinner at Earl Grey's, where most of the guests belonged to royal families. In fact, there was so much rank present that the Prime Minister of England was Number 99 at the dinner table. General

Greely was standing talking to two English ladies when Queen Mary came through the room toward them. Thinking she wished to speak to the ladies, General Greely stepped back, but she came straight over to him and engaged him in conversation. Greely was surprised that she remembered him but attributed it to the knee breeches episode!

On his first visit to England after his Polar trip, he had met and become very much attached to Mr. Gladstone and his family. Since then Mr. Gladstone had died, but his daughters, Helen Gladstone and Mary Gladstone Drew, invited General and Mrs. Greely to visit them. They saw Hawarden Castle again, were entertained extensively and attended service at the little church near by where they sat in the Gladstone pew. They visited the park, following the path by which Gladstone used to walk to morning service, and saw the oak grove where, in his vigorous days, he got his exercise chopping down trees.

He saw Lord Rosebery again, and his old friend, Sir Wilfrid Laurier, who, he felt, had done so much to bring about closer and more friendly relations between Canada and the United States. The Greelys were also entertained at luncheon in Windsor Castle.

Back in the United States, he turned his attention and remarkable energy to civic matters. It is not always easy for a retired army officer to fashion a new life for himself, but with General Greely there seemed no noticeable contrast in activity and enjoyment between his former life of active military service and that which he led after his retirement. His interests were many and varied. He wrote a great deal, something like a hundred articles of his on popular current topics having been published in magazines. Among his books were: "Three Years of Arctic Service"; "American Explorers and Travelers"; "True Tales of Arctic Heroism"; "Handbook of Arctic Discoveries"; "Handbook of Alaska"; "American Weather"; "Polar Regions in the Twentieth Century"; and "Reminiscences of Adventure and Service."

During the financial struggles of George Washington University, he accepted the unsalaried Chair of Geography, serving there several years. He was one of the charter members of the National Geographic Society and contributed throughout his life to its progress and success, being a member of the Board of Trustees continuously for 47 years.

On his eightieth birthday he was entertained at a party by Mr. Gilbert Grosvenor, President of the National Geographic Society, and Mrs. Grosvenor. Mrs. Grosvenor is the daughter of Prof. Alexander Graham Bell, inventor of the telephone. General Greely had known members of this family for five generations. It was he who had introduced Mrs. Grosvenor, then Elsie Bell, to her future husband, so he must be given credit for a successful piece of matchmaking among his other accomplishments.

He was one of the six original founders of the Cosmos Club of Washington. He also helped found a number of patriotic societies, such as the District of Columbia Sons of the Revolution, and was active in the work of the societies

of the Grand Army of the Republic, Loyal Legion, War of
1812, the Mayflower and the Carabaos. As an outgrowth of
these activities, he became a zealous supporter of a restric-
tive immigration policy, long before this was the accepted
thing it is today. He believed strongly in preserving the
homogeneity of the United States, feeling that the introduction of too great a body of certain alien elements threatened
the continued existence of our form of government.

His work toward giving Washington a public library and
developing the War Department library has already been
touched upon. In connection with this, a pleasant little anec-
dote came to light when General Greely's death was announced. A Washington newspaper man recalled that as a
small boy in the sixth grade, he had been given a theme to
write, which proved a very difficult task as he could not
obtain the necessary information from his parents or any
source available. Some one suggested that he go to the War
Department Library, which he did the following Saturday
morning. He found there a tall man with a graying beard and
a kindly eye, who placed himself at the service of the boy in
just the same manner as one would with a grown-up. The
boy explained his difficulty, and the tall man placed him at a
table and began to bring him book after book, all opened at
the right page to supply the needed information. Delighted,
the boy set to work. Soon lunchtime came and he asked his
kindly helper if he could come back later.

"You certainly may," was the reply, "possibly I shall be

out, but the books will be here waiting for you, and if you have any trouble, say that you are the visitor for whom General Greely reserved this table."

After the boy grew up, he saw a good deal of the famous soldier-explorer, but he likes best to remember him as the man who carried volume after volume from the shelves to help an unknown and discouraged youngster.

General Greely became interested in better housing for the poor and made himself an authority on the subject, working for it both by writing and lecturing. An address to the Chamber of Commerce of Reading, Pennsylvania, inspired them to start a campaign for improving the housing conditions of that city. On his seventieth birthday, a newspaper reporter came upon him "celebrating" the occasion by writing a magazine article on this subject.

In March, 1917, a little before Greely's 73rd birthday, Mrs. Greely died. She had been his inseparable companion and adviser for thirty-nine years and it was a severe blow to lose her; but with the same fortitude and philosophy that had supported him in past trials, he met this new one.

Shortly after her death, the old house on G Street was sold, and General Greely went to Cambridge, Massachusetts, to spend a year with his daughter Rose, who was finishing a course in architecture. He disposed of his famous Arctic library of more than 500 volumes to the National Geographic Society. It was a collection unique in this country, but he felt that as none of his children were Arctic experts, they were not the logical heirs to it; he wanted it to be where it could be consulted and utilized by explorers. He sent the rest of his books, papers, and personal effects to the summer place at Conway, where he lived every year from May well into November.

At the inception of the World War, General Greely was nearly ten years past the retiring age; so he could not take an active command in the field. However, with his old spirit and devotion, he wished to do anything possible to help the country. The Governor of Massachusetts, his native state, asked that he be placed on active duty for the purpose of directing the enlistment, equipping and training of the Massachusetts troops; but as the War Department had made it a rule not to permit any retired officer to be placed on active duty, the governor's request was not granted.

Greely has always kept up his connection with his old home state of Massachusetts. When Coolidge was Governor of the State, in 1918, and the Boston police strike occurred which brought him into national prominence, General Greely volunteered for duty as an ordinary policeman. Shortly after this, Coolidge introduced General Greely to the Massachusetts Legislature, calling their attention to the fact that Greely was one of the only two men who had ever been voted the "Thanks of the Commonwealth of Massachusetts."

In 1920, General Greely and his daughter were back in Washington, where Rose was establishing herself in business as a landscape architect. For two years they lived in an apartment on R Street; then Rose went to Europe for a year, during which time General Greely lived at the Cosmos Club. It was not until 1927 that General Greely settled in the Georgetown house, at 3131 O Street, that was his home until his death in 1935.

Chapter XVIII

LAST YEARS OF A TITAN

OF all his pursuits, exploration remained General Greely's paramount interest to the end. As the dean of Arctic explorers, he was consulted by every man of note who intended to lead a new expedition into polar zones. Besides those interested in Arctic work, he knew personally all the great explorers and scientists of the past two decades, as he knew those of the present time in many parts of the globe. He thought highly of Nansen, who was noted not only for the variety, unique experiences and success of his Arctic explorations, but also for distinction in other lines, as ambassador and scientist. It was his work in saving thousands of World War victims from starvation that especially excited General Greely's admiration. On one of his visits to America, General Greely presented him to the National Geographic Society. He also presented Evans, MacMillan, Mawson and others.

His association with Roald Amundsen, who discovered the South Pole, continued through many years, from the time of Amundsen's King William expedition to the north magnetic pole in 1903-06. He considered his work of exploration, in both the Arctic and Antarctic zones, unapproached in history. When Amundsen made his historic flight with Lincoln

Ellsworth in 1926 from Spitzbergen over the North Pole to Point Barrow, Alaska, he thus achieved the unique honor of having visited both the North and South Pole. It was after this that General Greely propounded the question to him, "Where does the magnetic needle point at the North Pole?" without obtaining a definite answer. He later asked this same question of Admiral Byrd, who replied in a courteous note saying that he did not have access to his records at the time but would undertake to answer the question later. But Greely heard no more from him about this.

"Nothing has been published as yet to my knowledge either from Peary, Byrd or Amundsen to show the true magnetic conditions at the North Pole," General Greely stated.

Some one asked him how the magnetic needle was really supposed to act at the Pole. He smiled and said, "Ah, if I knew myself, I would not have written to find out. Some say it should point south, others think it would point every way."

General Greely was Peary's earliest adviser when he first attacked the inland ice of Greenland, and naturally he was keenly interested in his exploits. When the controversy over Peary's claims was reopened in 1926, Greely was inevitably drawn into it. After a study of various analyses of Peary's records, he announced as his conclusion that he did not believe Peary had reached the Pole. He cited a number of inaccuracies of statement that would tend to disprove it, such as the proved non-existence of Crocker Land, which was demonstrated by Peary's assistant, MacMillan; and the discrediting of his reported discovery of Jesup Land, by the Navy Department.

"In his last journey," wrote General Greely, "when he traveled over difficult ice (as shown by his photographs), by compass where its declination was unknown, I cannot but deem his distances, location and times as often incorrect. . . . Unfortunately, similar inaccuracies of observation and statement were common in Peary's explorations."

There was also the fact that Peary had no scientific witness to substantiate his claim, as had Amundsen when he reached the South Pole. However, Greely pointed out that Peary should not be charged with intent to deceive.

"Of Peary as an explorer," he said, "I adhere to my earlier affirmations setting forth his indomitable courage, administrative ability and bulldog tenacity, his high qualities as a sledgeman, his persistence, unsurpassed in Arctic annals, and the value of his three remarkable records of unequaled northings. Science, however, demands absolute accuracy from explorers. But Pole or no Pole, Robert E. Peary stands first in his prolonged siege for the conquest of the North Pole."

Concerning Dr. Cook, General Greely was of the opinion that his field journey, covering fourteen continuous months, was an unsurpassed Arctic feat; but Cook's Polar claims he thought were likewise unsubstantiated.

Dr. Cook had been with Amundsen on several of his expeditions. When the noted Norwegian came to America several years ago for a lecture tour, he suddenly broke all engagements and sailed back to Europe. His reason for doing this remained a mystery for quite a while. It is now known that, prior to filling his lecture dates, he went to see Dr. Cook in the penitentiary at Leavenworth. His lecture manager, hearing of this, rushed to Amundsen and with no tact or understanding, upbraided him severely on the effect such fraternizing with "jail birds" would have on the success of his tour. "Americans would not understand it," he said. Amundsen explained that he had visited Dr. Cook as he would visit any of his men, no matter in what circumstances he found them. The upshot of it all was that Amundsen broke off relations with the lecture bureau, too much offended to continue even a profitable association with people who would take such a view of an act of kindness.

*   *   *   *   *

Of Byrd's flight over the Pole, General Greely said, "This flight insured beyond question priority by an American in attainment of that goal."

General Greely was past his eightieth year when Vilhjalmur Stefansson suggested to him that he revise his book, "Handbook of Arctic Discoveries." Instead of doing that, the General wrote an entirely new book, "The Polar Regions in the Twentieth Century, Their Discovery and Evolution," which was published in 1928. He took only four months to produce this work, writing it all himself on his typewriter, with one finger of each hand. He never employed a secretary for any of his work.

A very interesting story is told about Sven Hedin, the distinguished explorer who wrote so marvelously of his wanderings across Asia. General Greely was in London, attending the International Telegraph Conference, as representative of the United States, and, privately, the Institut Colonial International, of which he was one of the three active American members. A friend, Sir J. Scott Keltie, invited him to lunch to meet a well-known traveler, whose name he did not mention. It was none other than Sven Hedin, who was then editing the scientific results of his twenty years of Asiatic exploration, preparatory to further work. Hedin was very complimentary and charmed General Greely by telling him that he had especially wanted to meet one who had affected his life so materially. Upon General Greely's inquiring how that was, since they had never met, Hedin replied, "When I read your 'Three Years of Arctic Service,' I was so moved that I decided to devote my life to exploration. Asia is a contrast to the North Pole, but I hope that I have done my part therein and I shall die content if I earn as great fame as you have."

As all the world knows, Hedin continued to gain ever greater laurels for his daring exploits, until his untimely death in 1934.

In 1930 and 1931, General Greely discussed plans for the coming International Polar Year (1932) with Nansen and Sverdrup. At that time plans were being worked out for an American expedition of twenty men, under the leadership of Captain Flavel M. Williams, to spend two years at Fort

Conger, Ellesmere Island, where Greely and his men were stationed fifty years ago. This Arctic expedition, however, expected to be in constant touch with the United States by radio, and to traverse the vast stretches of ice fields by airplanes. Various contingencies later prevented the realization of these ambitious plans.

Sir Hubert Wilkins' project of crossing the Pole under the ice in a submarine was being widely discussed. General Greely shook his head over this, which struck him as an extremely dangerous adventure. "Wilkins has not seen that Arctic ice and I have," he said. "If he is actually planning a journey of several thousand miles under the ice, I am afraid we shall not see him again." He explained that while the general run of polar ice is from twelve to fourteen feet thick, there are great stretches of what are known as palæocrystic floes where the thickness ranges from thirty to several hundred feet. A submarine trapped under such a mass could hardly hope to break through it. It was undoubtedly fortunate for Sir Hubert that his plans had to be abandoned, when the submarine broke down on the way across the Atlantic Ocean, and had to be towed to port.

*　　　*　　　*　　　*　　　*

During his last few years, General Greely's physical activities were of necessity rather curtailed. Up to his 89th year, however, he continued to get around more or less as usual. Every afternoon about five he went down to the Cosmos

Club and played bridge with three old friends, returning home for dinner about seven.

He kept up a voluminous and very interesting correspondence with friends all over the world. Practically his only concession to advancing years was having breakfast in bed. He was usually dressed and downstairs by eleven o'clock, working at his writing or correspondence until lunch time. After that, he often worked again in the afternoon, until time to go to his club.

Until 1934, he took the trip north to his summer home alone. He stopped off first in Newburyport, Mass., to visit his relatives and old friends, arriving there for Decoration Day, when he marched in the parade with other G. A. R. veterans. He always said he would never go there when they got too old to march. There came a day when the old men were unable to make the grade and had to ride in an automobile in the parade. But General Greely, true to his word, did not go to Newburyport that year until after Decoration Day.

In 1927, General Greely wrote his memoirs, "Reminiscences of Adventure and Service"; while at the age of 84, in 1928, he brought out that remarkable book, "Polar Regions in the Twentieth Century," already mentioned. I know of no other work of a proportionate scope ever done by a man of eighty-four.

General Greely has known intimately the President of the United States and the mistresses of the White House for nearly seventy years. While he did not know President Lincoln, he saw him on two different occasions. From President Johnson's administration down to the present one, the doors of the Executive Mansion were open to him. Prior to his death on October 20, 1935, he was probably the only living person who had known intimately every one of importance in Washington from the time of the Civil War on, including all the Chief Justices from Chase to Hughes. Several years ago, Chief Justice Taft said, "I am glad to return to the only two permanent things in Washington: the Washington Monument and General Greely."

Once Greely was asked what was the most important and difficult work he had ever done, and he answered, "Bringing up six children on Army pay." Seriously speaking, however, he believes that his most interesting service and the one in which he thought he accomplished the most was in the earthquake at San Francisco.

An interesting sidelight on his character is the fact that he would never capitalize his Arctic experiences. Although he was offered many thousands of dollars to give lectures and make public appearances, he never accepted. How he felt about this, even forty years afterward, is set forth in a letter of his that appeared in the New York *Times* of January 1, 1924, in response to an article by Commander Fitzhugh Green, in the *Times* of December 30th. Commander Green had written, "When the Greely expedition went north forty years ago, the most finished program for support and relief was worked out that ever stood behind an Arctic expedition. It was openly said that the romance of exploration had been wiped out by too efficient management. Yet that expedition was one of the great tragedies of the past generation."

Excerpts from General Greely's reply are as follows:

The Greely expedition was an extraordinary success. The relief expeditions, managed from Washington, were ghastly failures. That 19 out of 25 of our men perished was due to the incompetency and to the desertion of the relief commands, both military and naval. . . . In my old age I cannot be disloyal even by silence to my dead, and allow misrepresentations to be spread unrefuted before the rising generation. The men of the Greely Expedition gave their lives in performing for the United States an international duty. Some think their success was a glory to America. . . . Returning penniless, I refused to appear on a public platform, though a small fortune was offered. Their blood and their sufferings have never been exploited for money or footlight fame. I rested on a record of duty done. I cannot fail to defend their fame. . . . Shortcomings are mine and they would be greater if I allowed these facts of international history to be distorted by placing on the memory of the dead a burden of responsibility that has already been placed on those who deserted a national command, leaving them to perish.

*　　　*　　　*　　　*　　　*

Sometime in January, 1935, in speaking about General Greely to some of his family and friends, I found that he had never received any special mark of favor or esteem from the United States Government. It occurred to me that this should be done at once. Accordingly, I saw Chairman Mc-

237

Swain of the House Military Affairs Committee, who was as astonished as I had been that General Greely had not received due recognition for his splendid services. Mr. McSwain introduced a bill into the House of Representatives, and Senator Joseph E. Robinson, the majority leader of the Senate, introduced a similar one in that body, which gave General Greely the Congressional Medal of Honor. This great distinction has been given to only two other men by Act of Congress.

The Medal was presented to Greely at his home in Georgetown by the Secretary of War, in the absence of the President of the United States, on his ninety-first birthday, March 27, 1935. The presentation of this medal was accompanied by a parade of troops, which greatly pleased General Greely. No detail of their arms, organization or appearance escaped him.

General Brainard was present, the only other surviving member of the Greely Arctic Expedition. It recalled to my mind what General Brainard had said about his old chief when he (Brainard) was presented with the American Geographical Society Charles P. Daly Medal in 1925, for exploration:

> This occasion gives me the opportunity of paying tribute to my commander in the North, General Greely. No more loyal, brave and resourceful officer ever commanded men in the Arctic regions or in any other place; his qualities as a leader of men rose to great heights during the closing days at Cape Sabine, when by his firmness and inflexible will he kept the remnant of the party together under military discipline to the hour of our

238

General Greely and General Brainard, on Greely's 91st Birthday

rescue by Admiral Schley. Through fifty years it has been my lot to observe military discipline administered in various ways, but never so kindly, firmly and effectively as on that memorable expedition.

The presentation of the Congressional Medal was acclaimed throughout the world and thousands of letters came to General Greely from many different countries, congratulating him on the belated honor which he so richly deserved.

I had a delightful talk with him only a few months before his death. His mind was as many-sided as ever. We discussed political and military conditions in Europe, about which his knowledge and judgment was thorough and penetrating, and he commented shrewdly and interestingly on the effect these things might have on the United States. About our own domestic situation, he had a few criticisms to make.

"I do not approve of much that is a part of the 'new deal,' " he said. "I believe that throughout the world people are becoming less civilized. We have had three wars in this country, the Civil, Spanish-American and World War. The Civil War was necessary, in my opinion, to preserve the Union, but what was the use of the other two? What was accomplished in either?

"We are suffering more and more today from mismanagement of affairs by the leading men in the country, particularly in financial fields. If they had been sensible, we would never have made the loans of eight or ten billions of dollars to European countries, now gone beyond any hope of recovery. That money would have been enough to keep our 10,000,000 idle men at work. How should they be put back to work? That is too large a problem for me. But certainly I should say it is wrong to pour out millions of dollars to people out of work, many of them because they won't work. You will be paying for this until you die. And surely it is wrong to urge farmers to stop growing food and to pay them millions of dollars to stop growing it, with millions of people claiming they are starving to death.

"People should be urged to live within their means.... If today's preachers would keep talking to their parishioners about economy, this would help, but the preachers are not doing their job in this regard."

General Greely always stated his views clearly and concisely on the subject of national defense. He believed in a strong defense, sufficient to protect the United States from any and all enemies, and had no use for the chronic pacifists.

He saw our country change from one of individual leadership to one handled by parties, firms, associations and societies, which might be termed "collectivism." He always gave a great deal of time and endeavor to helping any project which contributed to the patriotic, scientific or civic advantage of our country.

His great deeds were done years ago, and as many of our citizens, particularly the younger generation, have not had the opportunity of learning about them, I, as one of his old officers and great admirers, consider it a privilege to note some of the highlights of his remarkable career, in the hope that all Americans may become acquainted with the life of one of our greatest citizens. It should serve as an example of patriotism not only to us and to our children, but to our descendants as long as America lasts.

*   *   *   *   *

In the first days of October, 1935, General Greely was advised by his physicians to go to the Walter Reed Hospital, as his physical mechanism was showing signs of a break-up. There was nothing specifically the matter, but the whole machine of life had worn out and would soon cease to function. His mind was as clear, calm and composed as it had been all through his life. He died on October 20th, surrounded by his family.

A touching incident of his last days was the solicitous attention of General Brainard, now the sole survivor of the Greely Arctic expedition. General Brainard went to the hospital every day to see his old chief, and never for a moment would he admit, or even allow himself to think, that General Greely was going to die. "I have seen Greely much worse off than this and get through it," he insisted, "and I am sure he will do it again."

The last respects were tendered to this great man on October 22nd, when the caisson bearing his body moved slowly up the Fort Myer Road toward Arlington Cemetery, where he was laid to rest with the others of the nation's brave and distinguished servants. It was a day brilliant with sunshine and the bright, flaming colors of the autumn

241

leaves. As taps sounded, I was constrained to think of a desire he had expressed on one of his last birthdays, as he read letters of congratulation: "I hope I may never live to see a birthday when my faculties for enjoying these remembrances are impaired." He had his wish.